**SCHOLASTIC**
# ENGLISH SKILLS

# Spelling and vocabulary
## Year 5

**Recommended system requirements:**

Windows: XP (Service Pack 3), Vista (Service Pack 2), Windows 7 or Windows 8 with 2.33GHz processor
Mac: OS 10.6 to 10.8 with Intel Core™ Duo processor
1GB RAM (recommended)
1024 x 768 Screen resolution
CD-ROM drive (24x speed recommended)
Adobe Reader (version 9 recommended for Mac users)
Broadband internet connections (for installation and updates)

For all technical support queries (including no CD drive), please phone Scholastic Customer Services on 0845 6039091.

**Author**
Sally Burt and
Debbie Ridgard

**Editorial**
Rachel Morgan, Anna Hall,
Alison Cornwell and
Red Door Media

**CD-ROM design
and development**
Hannah Barnett, Phil Crothers,
and MWA Technologies Private Ltd

**Series design**
Shelley Best and Anna Oliwa

**Design team**
Nicolle Thomas and Andrea Lewis

**Illustrations**
Moreno Chiacchiera/Beehive Illustration

Scholastic Education, an imprint of Scholastic Ltd
Book End, Range Road, Witney, Oxfordshire, OX29 0YD
Registered office: Westfield Road, Southam,
Warwickshire CV47 0RA
www.scholastic.co.uk

Printed and bound by Ashford Colour Press
© 2016 Scholastic Ltd
1 2 3 4 5 6 7 8 9   6 7 8 9 0 1 2 3 4 5

**British Library Cataloguing-in-Publication Data**
A catalogue record for this book is available from
the British Library.
**ISBN 978-1407-14186-2**

FSC
www.fsc.org

MIX
Paper from
responsible sources
FSC® C011748

Extracts from The National Curriculum for England, English Programme of Study © Crown Copyright. Reproduced under the terms of the Open Government Licence (OGL). www.nationalarchives. gov.uk/doc/open-government-licence/version/3/

Every effort has been made to trace copyright holders for the works reproduced in this book, and the publishers apologise for any inadvertent omissions.

# Contents

## Chapter 1
### Revisit and reinforce

## Chapter 2
### Suffixes and prefixes

## Chapter 3
### Word endings

## Chapter 4
### Word families, roots and origins

## Chapter 5
### Homophones and other tricky words

## Chapter 6
### Improving your work

# Introduction

### Scholastic English Skills: Spelling and vocabulary

Learning to spell depends on much more than simply memorising words. Exercises, word lists and tests are not enough. Children need to actively engage in the process, tackling new words using knowledge and skills acquired, taking risks and making errors. Purposeful writing is a key to learning to spell. Children need to see spelling as a useful tool for communication (rather than a rod to be beaten with!). To study the spelling of words we need to take them out of context but context is needed to learn how to use them and to give purpose for using them. Children need to know more than just how to spell words, they need to know what they mean as well, as such spelling and vocabulary are intrinsically linked.

This series provides a bank of adaptable ideas and resources for teaching spelling and vocabulary. Each chapter is, to some extent, independent of the others and chapters do not, therefore, always need to be followed in order. Activities within a section sometimes build upon each other and should be followed sequentially. It is anticipated that sections and activities will be selected as required to fit in with medium-term planning for each term.

## Overview of the teaching of spelling and vocabulary

In English the relationship between sounds and letters (phonics) has been complicated by the complex history of the English language and there is not a simple one-to-one correspondence. Despite this complexity, a great deal of the relationship between letters and sounds is rule-bound, which means phonics works, but not all of the time. There is logic and pattern but there are also 'oddities'.

However spelling does not only represent sound; it also represents grammar and meaning. For example, the 'ed' suffix that identifies regular past-tense verbs can be pronounced 'd' or 'id' or 't' but never 'ed', but it is always spelled 'ed'. If spelling only represented sound, different accents would require different spellings. Instead of viewing the complexity as a problem, perhaps we might more usefully celebrate the richness and resourcefulness of English spelling.

Teaching spelling involves drawing children's attention to patterns: patterns of sounds and letters, patterns related to grammatical functions and patterns related to word origin. Although English spelling does have 'rules', such as 'q' is always followed by 'u', it is much more realistic to talk about patterns, conventions, possibilities and probabilities. Many so-called rules have so many exceptions or are so complex to explain, that they are not worth teaching. To teach something as a rule which is later contradicted is not helpful. Children become active, constructive learners by investigating and generalising common patterns, and acknowledging exceptions.

Vocabulary can be developed indirectly when children engage daily in oral language, listen to adults read to them and read extensively on their own. Vocabulary should also be taught directly both as individual words and word-learning strategies. Children need to develop curiosity about words and meanings. Good vocabulary teaching involves active engagement and fosters excitement about words, which leads to children attending more closely to them.

## About the product

This book contains activities for teaching spelling and vocabulary. Each chapter focuses on a different aspect of spelling knowledge or skills and is divided into sections. Each section includes teachers' notes – objective, background knowledge, notes on how to use the photocopiable pages, further ideas and digital content – and three photocopiable pages. Each chapter also features a poster and assessment section. At the end of the book you will find a glossary of terms, a word bank providing banks of words to be used in games and other activities, and general activities which provides a set of generic games, activities and circle times linked to the activities in this book.

## Posters

Each chapter has one poster. These posters are related to the content of the chapter and should be displayed and used for reference throughout the work on the chapter. The poster notes (on the chapter opening page) offer suggestions for how they could be used. There are black and white versions in the book and full-colour versions on the CD-ROM for you to print out or display on your whiteboard.

## Assessment

Each chapter concludes with an assessment section. It summarises the curriculum objectives and activities in the section, provides pointers on observation and record keeping and includes one assessment photocopiable page.

## Activities

Each section contains photocopiable page activities in the book. Each photocopiable page is also included on the CD-ROM for you to display or print out (answers are also provided, where appropriate, in a separate document on the CD-ROM).

Many of the photocopiable pages have linked interactive activities on the CD-ROM. These interactive activities are designed to act as starter activities to the lesson, giving whole-class support on the information being taught. However, they can also work equally well as plenary activities, reviewing the work the children have just completed.

## Workbooks

Accompanying this series is a set of workbooks containing practice activities which are divided into chapters to match the teacher's resource book. Use a combination of the photocopiable pages in this book and the activities in the workbook to help children practise and consolidate spelling and vocabulary skills.

## Differentiation

Activities in this book are not differentiated explicitly, although teacher notes may make suggestions for support or extension. Many of the activities can be used with the whole class with extra support provided through differentiated and open-ended questions, use of additional adults, mixed-ability paired or group work or additional input and consolidation before and/or after lessons. Some children may need support with the reading aspects of tasks in order to participate in the spelling objectives.

## Using the CD-ROM

Below are brief guidance notes for using the CD-ROM. For more detailed information, see 'How to use this digital content' on the Main menu.

The CD-ROM follows the structure of the book and contains:

- All of the photocopiable pages.
- All of the poster pages in full colour.
- Answers provided, where relevant.
- Interactive on-screen activities linked to the photocopiable pages.

## Getting started

Put the CD-ROM into your CD-ROM drive.

- For Windows users, the install wizard should autorun, if it fails to do so then navigate to your CD-ROM drive. Then follow the installation process.
- For Mac users, copy the disk image file to your hard drive. After it has finished copying double click it to mount the disk image. Navigate to the mounted disk image and run the installer. After installation the disk image can be unmounted and the DMG can be deleted from the hard drive.
- To install on a network, please see the ReadMe file located on the CD-ROM (navigate to your drive).

To complete the installation of the program you need to open the program and click 'Update' in the pop-up. Please note – this CD-ROM is web-enabled and the content will be downloaded from the internet to your hard-drive to populate the CD-ROM with the relevant resources. This only needs to be done on first use, after this you will be able to use the CD-ROM without an internet connection. If at any point any content is updated you will receive another pop-up upon start up with an internet connection.

## Main menu

The main menu is the first screen that appears. Here you can access: terms and conditions, registration links, how to use the digital content and credits. To access a specific year group click on the relevant button (NB only titles installed will be available). To browse all installed content click **All resources**.

## Chapter menu

The Chapter menu provides links to all of the chapters or all of the resources for a specific year group. Clicking on the relevant Chapter icon will take you to the section screen where you can access the posters and the chapter's sections. Clicking on **All resources** will take you to a list of all the resources, where you can search by keyword or chapter for a specific resource.

## Section menu

Here you can choose the relevant section to take you to its activity screen. You can also access the posters here.

## Activity menu

Upon choosing a section from the section menu, you are taken to a list of resources for that section. Here you can access all of the photocopiable pages related to that section as well as the linked interactive activities.

## All resources

All of the resources for a year group (if accessed via a Chapter menu) or all of the installed resources (if accessed via the Main menu). You can:

- Select a chapter and/or section by selecting the appropriate title from the drop-down menus.
- Search for key words by typing them into the search box.
- Scroll up or down the list of resources to locate the required resource.
- To launch a resource, simply click on the **Go** button.

## Navigation

The resources (poster pages, photocopiable pages and interactive activities) all open in separate windows on top of the menu screen. To close a resource, click on the **x** in the top right-hand corner of the screen and this will return you to the menu screen.

Closing a resource will not close the program. However, if you are in a menu screen, then clicking on the **x** will close the program. To return to a previous menu screen, you need to click on the **Back** button.

## Teacher settings

In the top left-hand corner of the Main menu screen is a small **T** icon. This is the teacher settings area. It is password protected, the password is: login. This area will allow you to choose the print quality settings for interactive activities 'Default' or 'Best'. It will also allow you to check for updates to the program or re-download all content to the disk via **Refresh all content**.

## Answers

The answers to the photocopiable pages can be found on the CD-ROM in the All resources menu. The answers are supplied in one document in a table-format, referencing the page number, title and answer for each relevant page. The pages that have answers are referenced in the 'Digital content' boxes on the teachers' notes pages. Unfortunately, due to the nature of English, not all pages can have answers provided because some activities require the children's own imaginative input or consist of a wider writing task.

# Objectives

| Page | Section | English skills objective | To use further prefixes and suffixes and understand the guidelines for using them. | To revise the use of the possessive apostrophe. (Years 3–4) | To continue to distinguish between homophones and other words which are often confused. | To convert nouns or adjectives into verbs using suffixes. (Grammar appendix) | To use verb prefixes. (Grammar appendix) | To use hyphens to avoid ambiguity. (Spelling appendix) | To use and spell endings 'cial' and 'tial' and 'cious' and 'tious'. (Spelling appendix) | To use and spell words ending in 'ant', 'ance', 'ent', 'ence' and 'ency'. (Spelling appendix) |
|---|---|---|---|---|---|---|---|---|---|---|
| 11 | Prefixes and suffixes | To practise using a range of prefixes and suffixes, understanding the guidance for adding them. | ✓ | | | | | | | |
| 15 | Suffixes and word endings | To add suffixes and choose word endings correctly. | ✓ | | | | | | | |
| 19 | Super spelling | To write sentences using sounds, words and punctuation taught so far. | | ✓ | ✓ | | | | | |
| 27 | Transforming words using suffixes | To convert nouns or adjectives into verbs using suffixes. | | | | ✓ | | | | |
| 31 | Verb prefixes | To use verb prefixes to transform verbs into other verbs with different meanings. | | | | | ✓ | | | |
| 35 | The hyphen | To understand the purpose of the hyphen and to begin to use it in spelling. | | | | | | ✓ | | |
| 43 | Which ending? | To spell words ending in 'cious' or 'tious'. | | | | | | | ✓ | |
| 47 | Rules and exceptions | To spell words ending in 'cial' or 'tial'. | | | | | | | ✓ | ✓ |
| 51 | Tricky letter strings | To spell words ending in 'ant'/'ance'/'ancy' and 'ent'/'ence'/'ency', making appropriate choices. | | | | | | | | ✓ |

Chapter 1: pages 11, 15, 19
Chapter 2: pages 27, 31, 35
Chapter 3: pages 43, 47, 51

# Objectives

# Chapter 1

# Revisit and reinforce

## Introduction

This chapter provides the children with the opportunity to revise elements of the curriculum covered in Years 3 and 4. They will revise the rules for adding prefixes and suffixes to root words and gain confidence in using spelling patterns. Spelling is not always simply absorbed, so providing the children with visual and auditory tools and practice is essential. Spelling a word is also not just about the letters and sounds in a word but about how the word is put together, hence understanding root words is fundamental to successful spelling. The children will also revise the possessive apostrophe in plural words, homophones and words from the Year 3 and 4 word lists. For further practice, please see the 'Revisit and reinforce' section in the Year 5 workbook.

## In this chapter

| Prefixes and suffixes page 11 | To practise using a range of prefixes and suffixes, understanding the guidance for adding them. |
| --- | --- |
| Suffixes and word endings page 15 | To add suffixes and choose word endings correctly. |
| Super spelling page 19 | To write sentences using sounds, words and punctuation taught so far. |
| Assessment page 23 | Activities and ideas to assess accuracy and confidence in spelling and punctuation. |

## Poster notes

### Super spelling starters (page 10)
The poster summarises the revision elements of the chapter. Remind the children that a root word (or base word) is the core but it can change its spelling and function as other parts are added. Discuss the meaning of the prefixes and suffixes, and what effect they have on the root word. Some suffixes change the word class: *swim* (verb) – *swimmer* (noun); some change the tense: *call* (present) – *called* (past); some change the status of the word: *coin* (singular) – *coins* (plural). When the plural becomes possessive, remind them to add the apostrophe 's'. Ask the children to use the homophones in a sentence.

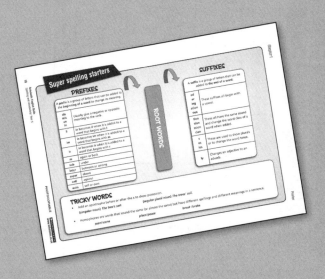

# Super spelling starters

## PREFIXES

A **prefix** is a group of letters that can be added to the **beginning of a word** to change its meaning.

| | |
|---|---|
| dis<br>mis<br>un<br>in | Usually give a negative or opposite meaning to the verb. |
| il | in becomes **il** when it is added to a word that begins with **l** |
| im | in becomes **im** when it is added to a word that begins with **m** |
| ir | in becomes **ir** when it is added to a word that begins with **r** |
| re | again or back |
| sub | under |
| inter | between or among |
| super | above |
| anti | against |
| auto | self or own |

## ROOT WORDS

## SUFFIXES

A **suffix** is a group of letters that can be added to **the end of a word**.

| | |
|---|---|
| ed<br>er<br>ing<br>ation<br>ous | These suffixes all begin with a vowel. |
| tion<br>sion<br>ssion<br>cian | These all have the same sound and change the word class of a word when added. |
| s<br>es<br>ies | These are used to show plurals or to change the word tense. |
| ly | Changes an adjective to an adverb. |

## TRICKY WORDS

- Add an apostrophe before or after the **s** to show possession.

  (singular noun) *The tree's soil.*                    (regular plural noun) *The trees' soil.*

- Homophones are words that sound the same (or almost the same) but have different spellings and different meanings in a sentence.

  *seen/scene*                    *piece/peace*                    *break/brake*

**Scholastic English Skills**
Spelling and vocabulary: Year 5

# Prefixes and suffixes

## Objective

To practise using a range of prefixes and suffixes, understanding the guidance for adding them.

## Background knowledge

In previous years the children learned some rules about how to add prefixes and suffixes to root words. Here are a few generalised rules to guide the children. Use the following rules to add negative prefixes:
- **'un' and 'in':** These prefixes can be added to most root words with no change to the spelling. For example, *happy – unhappy, possible – impossible.*
- **'il', 'im', 'ir' (variations of 'in'):** Words beginning with 'l' add the prefix 'il' (*legal – illegal*). Words beginning with 'm' add the prefix 'im' (*mortal – immortal*). Words beginning with 'r' add the prefix 'ir' (*rational – irrational*).
- **'dis' and 'mis':** These prefixes can be added to most root words with no change to the spelling. For example, *satisfied – dissatisfied, understand – misunderstand.*
Use the following rules to add prefixes that begin with a vowel letter:
- **'ing', 'er', 'ed':** If the word has more than one syllable, the last syllable is stressed, and it ends with one consonant only, the consonant is doubled. For example, *forget – forgetting, occur – occurred.*
- **'ous':** If the root word is obvious, the usual rules apply for adding suffixes beginning with vowel letters. for example, *poisonous, various, famous.*

## Activities

- **Photocopiable page 12 'A negative experience'**
As the children change a passage from positive to negative by adding negative prefixes, they reinforce their knowledge of the spelling patterns when adding 'dis', 'mis', 'in', 'il', 'im', 'ir', 'un'. They extend their vocabulary further by finding synonyms for the words with negative prefixes. Ask volunteers to read the passage aloud with their alternative words.

- **Photocopiable page 13 'Prefixes sorted'**
The children match the given prefixes with their meanings. In the previous activity, the children saw how prefixes can create antonyms. In this activity, the learners see how adding a prefix can also create a new word.
- **Photocopiable page 14 'All aboard the suffix train'**
Revise syllabification so that the children remember how to identify the number of syllables in a word. The number of syllables in a word is the number of vowel sounds heard. Generally speaking, if there are two middle consonants, split between them (*mud/dle*); divide before a single middle consonant (*o/pen*) and divide compounds, prefixes, suffixes and root words. Revise the rule for adding a suffix to the end of a word.

## Further ideas

- **Prefix and suffix cards:** Make prefix and suffix cards to add to root word cards. Play games where the children need to add prefixes, suffixes or both to make new words. They can play in pairs or small groups.
- **Spin a word web:** Make an interactive poster showing a spider diagram with different prefixes in the centre. Words must be added to sections of the web grouping words with the same prefix or suffix. Encourage the children to add words to the web as they come across them and let the web grow.
- **Find the roots:** Give the children a list of words that have a prefix and/or a suffix like 'unimpressed' and 'inconsiderate'. Invite them to find the root word by removing the parts that have been added. Let them use a dictionary to find or check their answers.

## Digital content

On the digital component you will find:
- Printable versions of all three photocopiable pages.
- Answers to all three photocopiable pages.
- Interactive versions of 'A negative experience' and 'Prefixes sorted'.

Name:

## Prefixes and suffixes

# A negative experience

■  Use prefixes to change a recount of a holiday from positive to negative (for example *polite* would become *impolite*). Write the new words in the spaces. Use these prefixes: **dis, mis, in, il, im, ir, un**.

Last summer, my trip to the seaside with my family was really _____pleasant.

My uncle was very _____patient and _____agreeable the whole

time. My aunt was terribly _____organised, probably because she was

so _____enthusiastic about everything. My cousins were _____sociable and

constantly _____obedient which made the whole trip totally _____bearable.

They _____behaved like _____mature, _____responsible playmates.

I _____liked the hotel where we stayed and found the food _____edible. In

future, family holidays with them will be _____regular events, if I can help it!

■  Fill in the suitcase on the left with five negative words you have made.

■  Find an alternative word for each (such as *dull* or *boring* instead of *unexciting*) and put them in the other suitcase.

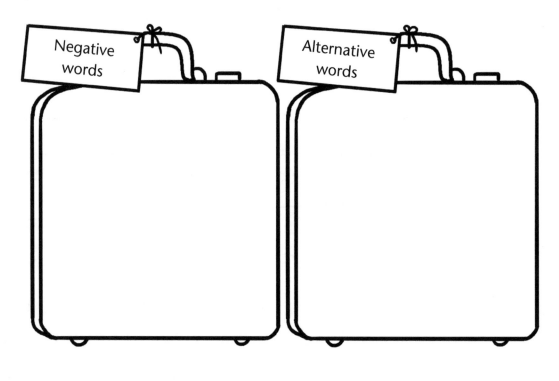

Negative words

Alternative words

**PHOTOCOPIABLE**   **SCHOLASTIC** www.scholastic.co.uk

# Prefixes and suffixes

# Prefixes sorted

■ Write the correct prefix next to each of the meanings below.

| re    sub    inter    super    anti    auto |
|---|

| Prefix | Meaning |
|---|---|
|  | Under |
|  | Above |
|  | Again or back |
|  | Against |
|  | Between or among |
|  | Self or own |

■ Change the words in the word bank by adding one of the above prefixes. Write the new words in the boxes below.

| position | consider | sonic | zero | social | climax |
|---|---|---|---|---|---|

build        merge        national        clockwise

standard        group        graph

natural        market        change        mobile        biography

| Re | Sub |
|---|---|
|  |  |
| Inter | Super |
|  |  |
| Anti | Auto |
|  |  |

## Prefixes and suffixes

# All aboard the suffix train

| occur | mention | forget | begin | prefer |
|---|---|---|---|---|

consider      question      danger      disappear

poison      appal      mountain

■ Work out which syllable is stressed in the words above. Sort the words onto the correct train, and then add one of the suffixes below onto each word.

ing    er    ed    ous

**Boarding the first train:** Calling all words with the final syllable stressed.
Please double the final consonant before adding an appropriate suffix from the list.

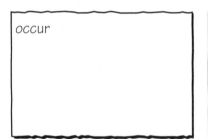

occur

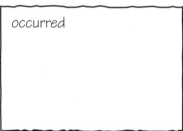

occurred

**Boarding the second train:** Calling all words with the final syllable unstressed.
Please do not double the final consonant before adding an appropriate suffix.

mention

mentioned

■ Complete the sentences below using these new words.

1. I have _____ all my options.

2. The teacher _____ marking the short answers.

3. She kept _____ to bring her homework in.

4. The nervous magician was a _____ at doing tricks.

5. The final test results were _____.

**Scholastic English Skills**
**14** Spelling and vocabulary: Year 5          PHOTOCOPIABLE      ■SCHOLASTIC
www.scholastic.co.uk

# Suffixes and word endings

## Objective

To add suffixes and choose word endings correctly.

## Background knowledge

These photocopiable pages reinforce the use of some of the suffixes and word endings covered in Years 3 and 4. A suffix is a group of letters added onto the end of a word to change the way you use it. Adding a suffix can change the class of a word (from verb to noun), the tense of a word (from present to past) or the status of a word (from singular to plural). The spelling of a suffix never changes but the spelling of the word to which it is added may change, depending on the root word's ending. This section is a good opportunity to deal with any confusion as some word endings sound the same such as 'tion'/'sion'/'ssion'/'cian'. The children will be given the opportunity to drill some of these rules but it is also important that they use the words in a sentence.

## Activities

● **Photocopiable page 16 'Noun-ation'**
Remind the children that when you add a suffix beginning with a vowel ('ation') to root words ending with an 'e' after a consonant, you drop the 'e'. Use examples from the classroom of action words that might be changed to nouns by adding 'ation', for example *dictate* becomes *dictation*. Discuss other words in the same word family (*dictation, dictate, diction* and *dictionary*) and encourage them to increase their vocabulary.

● **Photocopiable page 17 'Shhh!'**
These suffixes were introduced in Year 4. Ask the children if they can remember any rules they learned. They might recall the following: 'tion' is the most common and is used if the root ends in 't' or 'te'; 'ssion' is used if the root ends in 'ss' or 'mit'; 'sion' is used if the root ends in 'd'/'de' or 's'/'se' (with exceptions *attend/*

*attention* and *intend/intention*); 'cian' is used if the root ends in 'c' or 'cs'. Let them use their prior knowledge to sort the words into the correct categories and write them out correctly.

● **Photocopiable page 18 'What's buzzing?'**
This activity relies on correct pronunciation of the words. Make sure you give everyone an opportunity to hear and say the words correctly. Even though the sound is slightly different, the rule remains the same (as provided above) for adding the suffix. The children sort the words into groups showing the correct sound and then use some of the words in sentences.

## Further ideas

● **Change the word class:** Display a word and say what word class it is. (*She is a happy person – happy is an adjective.*) The children must add a prefix or suffix to the word to change its function and use it in a sentence as a different word class. (*Her happiness was obvious when she won the prize. Abstract noun.*)
● **What do you want to be?:** Ask the children to think of occupations that end with the suffix 'cian'. Begin with words already provided on the photocopiable sheet (like *magician, electrician, musician*).
● **The 'buzz game':** You will need to use an area where there is space for the children to run. One side of the room represents the /shun/ sound and one side represents the /zhun/ sound. Display a word and the children must run to the correct side of the classroom. Anyone who runs in the wrong direction is out.

## Digital content

On the digital component you will find:
● Printable versions of all three photocopiable pages.
● Answers to all three photocopiable pages.
● Interactive version of 'Noun-ation' and 'Prefixes sorted'.

Name:

# Noun-ation

■ A root word has been used in each sentence as a verb. Add the suffix **ation** to change the word to a noun and then use it to complete the sentence.

**Tip:** For root words ending with a consonant, simply add **ation**. For words that end with **e**, drop it.

1. The instructor will **inform** you by reading the important _____information_____.

2. Please **confirm** your appointment by sending me your _____.

3. He must be sure to **medicate** with the correct amount of _____.

4. To **prepare** for your test you should complete the _____.

5. From the _____ of his fans it is clear that they **adore** him.

6. We use electronic _____ to **communicate** with everyone.

7. **Interpret** the article, then give me your _____ of the events.

8. Your _____ will improve if you **punctuate** your work carefully.

■ Write the words in the box below and think of other words from the same family. Use a dictionary to help you.

| The verb | The noun | Other words in the family |
|----------|----------|---------------------------|
| Inform | Information | Informative |
| | | |

## Suffixes and word endings

# Shhh!

All of these suffixes have the /**sh**/ sound.

■ Some words have fallen asleep and lost their endings. Read the bedtime rules then send the words back to their own beds. The first one has been done for you.

**Bedtime rules**

If the root word ends in **t** or **te**, add **tion**.
If the root word ends in **ss** or **mit**, add **ssion**.
If the root word ends in **c** or **cs**, add **cian**.
If the root word ends in **d** or **se**, add **sion** (exceptions *magician* and *politician*).

tense
magic
~~discuss~~ electric
invent perfect possess music
compress subtract suppress
promote comprehend
hesitate optic extend express
submit expand frustrate regress

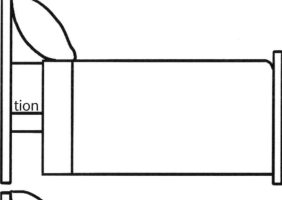

tion

sion

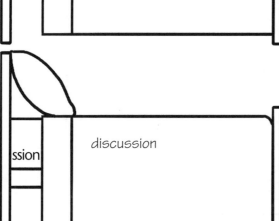

ssion    *discussion*

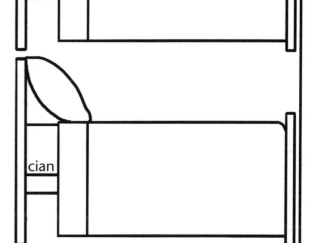

cian

■ Use nouns from the lists above to complete the following sentences.

1. The scientist was excited about his latest _____.

2. In maths we do lots of addition and _____.

3. Playing a sport is a good way to relieve stress, _____ and _____.

4. A group _____ is a good opportunity for self-_____.

**Suffixes and word endings**

# What's buzzing?

**Tip:** Sometimes the suffix **sion** makes a /**shun**/ sound and sometimes it makes a /**zhun**/ sound.

■ Say each word aloud. Can you hear the buzz? Write **shun** or **zhun** next to each word to show what sound you hear.

television  _____          tension  _____

abrasion  _____          fusion  _____

pollution  _____          possession  _____

condition  _____          suppression  _____

■ Cross out the words that are in the incorrect box and send them back to where they belong by writing them in the correct box.

| /shun/ | /zhun/ |
|---|---|
| expansion | revision |
| supervision | division |
| confusion | invasion |
| comprehension | tension |
| collision | persuasion |
| television | extension |

■ Use the incorrectly placed words to complete the following sentences.

1. Please ensure there is adult _____ at the party.

2. I love to watch _____ with my friends.

3. There was much _____ when the train did not arrive.

4. There was a terrible _____ on the road.

5. When I walked into the room I could feel the _____.

# Super spelling

## Objective

To write sentences using sounds, words and punctuation taught so far.

## Background knowledge

The photocopiable pages in this final revision section cover a variety of aspects from the Year 3 and 4 curriculum. One of the most tricky punctuation rules is how to use apostrophe 's' to show possession. Teachers often find apostrophe 's' used randomly and excessively. The children revise the use of the apostrophe 's', specifically in possessive plurals, and use the words in context. Remind the children of the difference between regular plural nouns (those that end with 's' or 'es') and irregular plural nouns (those that do not end with 's' or 'es'). To improve vocabulary and spelling, the children recall homophones covered in previous years. They focus on choosing the correct word for meaning and context and use it according to its word class. The last photocopiable page deals with tricky words that rhyme but do not look the same. Pronunciation is key so children should be given time to practise the words orally.

## Activities

● **Photocopiable page 20 'Lost property'**
This revises the possessive apostrophe with plural words. In Year 4 the children learned how to use apostrophe 's' with singular and regular plural nouns (*boys – boy's – boys'*) and how to use the apostrophe with irregular plurals (*children – children's*). The apostrophe is always placed after the plural form of the word. Remind the children that the apostrophe of possession is different from the apostrophe of omission which is used in contractions (*it's, can't, I've*).
● **Photocopiable page 21 'Homophones rain hear'**
Before showing the photocopiable sheet to the children, ask them if they remember the meaning of 'homophone' and invite some examples. Display their words on the board and invite them to add to it with

words not found on the photocopiable sheet. Listen out for incorrect pronunciation, reminding them that some homophones sound exactly the same (*bough/bow*) while some have slight differences in sound. Let them think of examples of near homophones whose meanings are often confused (*accept/except, affect/effect*).
● **Photocopiable page 22 'Snap! That sounds the same'**
The children use the words provided to revise some of the tricky sounds and letter strings covered in Years 3 and 4. Many words from the Year 3 and 4 lists have been used; you can also encourage them to find their own words to add to the activity. Use the photocopiable sheet in a way that suits you – drawing lines to connect words, colour coding or cutting and pasting into books all work well. You could ask the children to recall any rules they've learned to remind them how to spell these words.

## Further ideas

● **Design it:** Give the children the chance to design their own crossword using homophones as the answers. They must design the clues.
● **Pick and choose:** Keep a homophone box/jar in the class. Ask the children to look out for interesting homophones in their readers or daily conversations. As they find words, they should write them down and add them to the box/jar. At random times, give someone a chance to dip into the box, choose a homophone and then pick on a friend to make up sentences.
● **Competition time:** Make revision fun by holding a class spelling competition using the tricky words covered in this section. Put the children in teams and give each child a chance to spell a word and earn a point for their team. Words should be given in context and competitors should be given the chance to write the word down before spelling it out.

## Digital content

On the digital component you will find:
● Printable versions of all three photocopiable pages.
● Answers to all three photocopiable pages.
● Interactive version of 'Homophones rain here'.

Name:

## Super spelling

# Lost property

My pupils' homework is lost – we can't find it anywhere!

And which pupil might that be?

The whole class!

■ Return this lost property to the correct owners. Write a short sentence to show who owns what. The first two have been done for you.

| caps | dolls | files | milk | tickets | toys |
|---|---|---|---|---|---|
| | make-up | tails | cage | kennel | |

LOST PROPERTY BOX

| Regular plurals ending in **s** get **s'** | | Irregular plurals not ending with **s** get **'s** | |
|---|---|---|---|
| boys | The boys' caps. | children | The children's toys. |
| girls | | women | |
| teachers | | deer | |
| cats | | mice | |
| dogs | | men | |

■ Tick the sentences that show the plural possessive form.
- ☐ The car's tyres were smooth and slippery on the wet roads.
- ☐ The sheep's grass is green and lush.
- ☐ The cleaners' equipment was packed away.
- ☐ The principal's files are missing.
- ☐ The newspapers' headlines were very interesting.
- ☐ The men's boots lay on the ground.
- ☐ The trees' colours turned quickly when autumn arrived.

# Super spelling

# Homophones rain hear

**Tip:** Homophones are words that sound the same but they have different meanings or functions in a sentence.

■ Circle the verb in each set of words and then use the verb in your own sentence. You can write your sentences on the back of this sheet.

| ball/bawl | grate/great | here/hear | he'll/heal |
|-----------|-------------|-----------|------------|
| medal/meddle | missed/mist | rain/reign | scene/seen |
| weight/wait | ate/eight | see/sea | heard/herd |

■ Cross out the incorrect word in each sentence.

1. I'll **accept**/**except** your invitation.

2. I can eat everything **accept**/**except** eggs.

3. The rules will **affect**/**effect** everyone.

4. Coloured lights will be used for **affect**/**effect**.

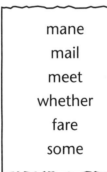

■ Find the matching homophones in the boxes below. Then use the nouns from each pair to complete the sentences below.

| | |
|---|---|
| meat | mane |
| fair | mail |
| male | meet |
| weather | whether |
| main | fare |
| sum | some |

1. Please buy some red _____ for supper tonight.

2. We'll be going to the country _____ on Saturday.

3. The activity for today depends on sunny _____.

4. I brushed the horse's _____.

5. You can do that _____ with a calculator.

Name:

## Super spelling

# Snap! That sounds the same

■ When words are difficult to read and pronounce, it helps to know how they should sound. Cut out the cards below and arrange them into pairs that have the same sound, like *weight/straight*.

■ Try adding your own tricky words with the same sounds on the blank cards.

■ You can also use the cards to play snap with a partner.

| | | | |
|---|---|---|---|
| weight | length | injection | throw |
| enough | February | builder | extension |
| strength | height | through | breathe |
| caught | tough | though | exercise |
| fright | thought | believe | doctor |
| century | straight | surprise | continue |
| much | touch | famous | various |
| | | | |
| | | | |

PHOTOCOPIABLE

# Assessment

## Assessment grid

The following grid shows the main objectives and activities covered in this chapter. You can use the grid to locate activities that cover a particular focus that you are keen to monitor.

| Objectives | Page | Activity title |
|---|---|---|
| To use further prefixes and suffixes and understand the guidelines for using them. | 12<br>13<br>14<br><br>16<br>17<br>18 | A negative experience<br>Prefixes sorted<br>All aboard the suffix train<br>Noun-ation<br>Shhh!<br>What's buzzing? |
| To revise the use of the possessive apostrophe. | 20 | Lost property |
| To continue to distinguish between homophones and other words which are often confused. | 21<br>22 | Homophones rain hear<br>Snap! That sounds the same |

## Observation and record keeping

For those still struggling with these prefixes, let them find words with prefixes in their readers. Take note of who is easily able to handle the photocopiable sheets in this section and who needs assistance. Identify children who still don't understand what a 'syllable' is or struggle to hear the tricky /shun/ or /zhun/ sounds. Place them in groups and work with them orally. The children should be clear on the difference between an apostrophe of possession and an apostrophe of omission. Be aware of children who add the apostrophe randomly in their written work.

## Assessment activity

● **What you need**
Photocopiable page 24 'Show what you know', writing materials.
● **What to do**
Hand out the photocopiable sheet and show the children the six different categories. Ask them to remember an example of each one and share it with the class. Once they have recalled the various areas covered, let them work through the photocopiable sheet on their own. They should read the simple text provided and identify the mistakes. Once they have circled the mistakes, they must classify them. The text is simple to allow them to focus on the task.

## Differentiation

● For those who need extra assistance, help them to get started by reading through the text and helping them to identify the errors. For some children, this will be enough and they will manage the rest on their own. For others, you may need to work through one example for each category as set out in the answer grid.

## Further learning

● **My pet:** The children can write a personal story about their own pet. Challenge them to include language from all the categories in the photocopiable page and to underline the words to show where they are in the text.

Name:

## Assessment

# Show what you know

■ Read the following passage and circle the errors. Then write the correct words in one of the boxes below.

**Remember** – don't confuse the contraction *it's* and the possessive *its*.

I have a special pet – a hamster. Its a nocturnal pet so it sleeps during the day and plays around in its cage at night. Hamster's front teeth are large and sharp for gnawing and their fur is very soft and warm. Althow my hamsters cage is small, it's comfortable with a wheel to ensure it gets enouff exercise. Hamsters use their cheek's to store and carry food so theres' never a shortage of that!

One day I left the cages' door wide open and my hamster escaped. He headed strait for the pantry. Ate days later we found him nesting in a box of old packet's. Since that weeks' event, I call him The Bandit. The next time The Bandit disappeared, it was one of my classmates' fault. I took him to school for Show & Tell. I thougt he was safe but someone left the cage open and off he went! You should've herd the children's noise! I finally cauhtg him and returned him to safety. Hes a grate pet to have.

| Plural | Singular possessive | Plural possessive |
|---|---|---|
|  |  |  |
| Contraction | Homophone | Tricky gh sounds |
|  |  |  |

# Chapter 2

# Suffixes and prefixes

This chapter covers using prefixes and suffixes to transform words, particularly to form verbs, as well as introducing the role of the hyphen. Children practise using suffixes to change the word class of a root word, for example from nouns or adjectives into verbs, while also applying relevant spelling rules. They add both prefixes and suffixes to root words to create new words, drawing on their familiarity with the sounds of words to select the correct prefix ('dis', 'de', 'mis', 'over', 're'). The children also learn the value of the hyphen when adding prefixes to verbs to aid pronunciation and clarify meaning. For further practice, please see the 'Suffixes and prefixes' section in the Year 5 workbook.

## In this chapter

| | |
|---|---|
| **Transforming words using suffixes** page 27 | To convert nouns or adjectives into verbs using suffixes. |
| **Verb prefixes** page 31 | To use verb prefixes to transform verbs into other verbs with different meanings. |
| **The hyphen** page 35 | To understand the purpose of the hyphen and to begin to use it in spelling. |
| **Assessment** page 39 | Activities and ideas to assess use of prefixes and suffixes. |

## Poster notes

**Transforming words with suffixes and prefixes (page 26)**

Use the poster to reinforce the meaning of adjectives, nouns and verbs, and to demonstrate adding suffixes beginning with a vowel. Invite a child to explain the meaning of one of the root words from the top of the poster. Discuss its word class and demonstrate how adding a suffix transforms it into a verb. Invite volunteers to choose which suffix to add to the other verbs by experimenting with which suffix sounds correct. Encourage the use of dictionaries to check and point out any spelling rules. Use the bottom part of the poster to show how prefixes can transform verbs into new verbs with a different meaning. Explain the meaning of the prefixes by comparing the meaning of the base verb and the prefixed verb.

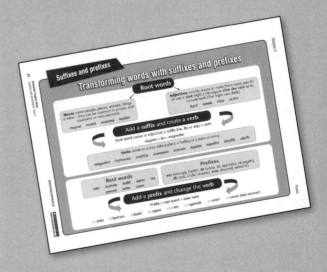

# Suffixes and prefixes

# Transforming words with suffixes and prefixes

## Root words

**Nouns** name people, places, animals, things or ideas – they can be common or proper, and countable or non-countable.

*magnet   mobile   economy   hyphen*

**Adjectives** modify nouns to make them more specific (It was a *dark* night.) OR appear **after the verb** as its complement (The night was *dark*.)

*legal   simple   clear   active*

### Add a suffix and create a verb

Root word (noun or adjective) + suffix (ise, ify or ate) = verb

*magnet + ise = magnetise*

**Verbs** name an action taking place, a feeling or a state of being.

*magnetise   hyphenate   mobilise   economise   activate   legalise   equalise   simplify   clarify*

## Prefixes

**mis** (wrongly, badly), **de** (undo, do opposite), **re** (again), **dis** (not, undo, reverse), **over** (beyond, extreme)

### Add a prefix and change the verb

Prefix + root word = new verb

### Root words

*take   hydrate   build   agree   see   operate   enter   cover*

*mistake   dehydrate   rebuild   disagree   oversee   co-operate   re-enter   re-cover (not recover)*

# Transforming words using suffixes

## Objective

To convert nouns or adjectives into verbs using suffixes.

## Background knowledge

Some suffixes change the word class of the root or base word they are added to. In this section, the children explore how the suffixes 'ate', 'ify', 'ise' and 'en' change nouns or adjectives into verbs: *class – classify*; *magnet – magnetise*; *facility – facilitate*; *dark – darken*. The suffixes 'ise' and 'ify' mean to become, to cause to be or to make; 'en' also means to cause to be, whereas 'ate' means to give the thing or quality mentioned. Some base words belong to several word classes (for example, *dead*) so it would be useful to explain, using a dictionary, how words can have multiple meanings and therefore be verbs, nouns, adverbs and so on, according to contextual use. It is also worthwhile exploring which suffixes fit which base words and thinking why *deadise* sounds wrong. The activities will remind children that adding certain suffixes may modify the base word spelling, for example, 'e' or 'y' is dropped when adding suffixes beginning with a vowel. Discuss the rules and changes with the children.

## Activities

● **Photocopiable page 28 'Action suffixes'**
Share the noun and verb definitions with the children to ensure they can easily differentiate them before tackling the activities. Contextualise the learning by making up sentences together that include new verbs created by the various suffixes ('ise', 'ify' and 'ate'). As a plenary activity, write this list of verbs on the board: *mummify*, *identify*, *fabricate*, *glaciate*, *advertise* and *categorise*. Draw up two columns, headed 'noun' and 'suffix', and ask the children to help break each word into its constituent parts.

● **Photocopiable page 29 'Pot luck'**
In this activity the children need to identify the adjectives in the pot and then transform them into verbs using the suffixes 'ise', 'ify', 'ate' and 'en'. Check they are comfortable with the adjective definitions before starting. Follow up by challenging the children to write definitions for four of the new verbs.

● **Photocopiable page 30 'Make me a verb'**
Deepen the children's understanding of why these suffixes create verbs by explaining their meaning, for example *classify* makes a noun become part of a class or group. Note other word classes can also end in 'ate' (*fortunate*, *electorate* and so on). Ask them to add 'ise' to *critic* and *television*. Discuss what happens to the sound of the root word in *criticise* (hard 'c' to soft 'c' because followed by 'i') and the spelling of the root in *televise* ('ision' replaced with 'ise').

## Further ideas

● **Pairs:** Make card pairs of various root words and appropriate suffixes to play 'pairs'. This game strengthens the children's memory skills and makes them think carefully about which suffix goes with which root word.

● **Making words:** Use the poster on page 26 and give the children a selection of root words to see if they can create verbs by adding the suffixes. How did they arrive at the correct spelling? What spelling rules did they apply?

● **Search for the root:** Note any uses of verbs with the suffixes 'ate', 'ify', 'ise' and 'en' in your reading or classwork. Ask the children to identify the root word, noting any spelling changes either at the end or in the middle of the root word.

## Digital content

On the digital component you will find:
● Printable versions of all three photocopiable pages.
● Answers to all three photocopiable pages.
● Interactive version of 'Make me a verb'.

Name:

# Action suffixes

| **What is a noun?** | **What is a verb?** |
|---|---|
| Nouns are naming words: they name people, places, animals, things or ideas. They can be common or proper, and countable or non-countable. | Verbs can be action or doing words because they name actions, but they can also name states or feelings. |

■ Choose the right suffix to get these nouns into action. Remember that you may need to follow a spelling rule as the suffixes begin with a vowel. Write your new verbs in the box and use a dictionary to check them.

Remember, you'll often need to get rid of a **y** or lose an **e** from the root word before you add the suffix.

| Nouns | Suffixes to choose from | New verbs |
|---|---|---|
| author | ate | authorise |
| character | ify | |
| hyphen | ise | |
| apology | | |
| standard | | |
| assassin | | |
| note | | |
| individual | | |
| class | | |
| symbol | | |

■ Separate each verb into its root noun + suffix, and then underline where the root word's spelling changed when the suffix was added.

| Verbs | Noun | Suffix |
|---|---|---|
| horrify | horr<u>or</u> | ify |
| pollinate | | |
| exemplify | | |
| justify | | |
| aerate | | |
| televise | | |

## Transforming words using suffixes

# Pot luck

> **Adjectives** modify a noun to make it more specific (*It was a **dark** night.*)
> OR appear after the verb *be* as its **complement** (*The night was **dark**.*)

■ Find all the adjectives in the pot and cook them up with one of the suffixes under the pot to form verbs. Write these verbs on the menu below. Remember to apply spelling rules to get your verb just right.

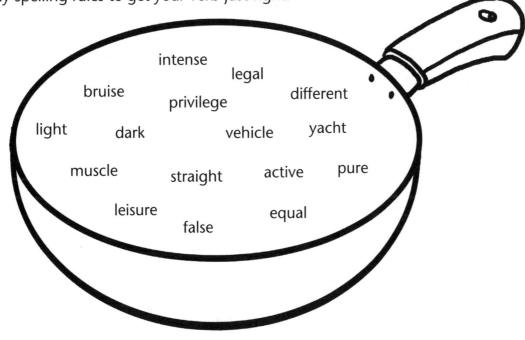

intense
legal
bruise
privilege
different
light
dark
vehicle
yacht
muscle
straight
active
pure
leisure
equal
false

**Suffixes:** ify   ise   ate   en

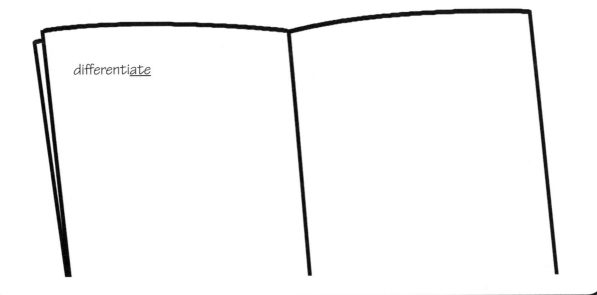

differentiate

**Transforming words
using suffixes**

# Make me a verb

■  A root word has been used in each sentence (in bold). Write in the brackets whether the root word is a noun, adjective or adverb.

■  Add one of the suffixes below to each root word and create a verb to write on the line. The first one has been done for you.

| | | | |
|---|---|---|---|
| ate | ify | ise | en |

1. The **vandal** (noun) threw stones at the bus stop; he was going to *vandalise* it because he was bored.

2. The maths problem was quite **simple** (                ) but the teacher tried to

_____ it even further, so that everyone could work out the answer.

3. The **magnet** (               ) had stopped attracting the iron filings, so Ted

tried to _____ it again.

4. Lauren painted the sky a **light** (               ) blue and then tried to

_____ it further by adding a white wash to it.

5. The police did not know the **identity** (               ) of the thief, so the

victim had to _____ him in a line up.

6. The **medic** (               ) arrived at the scene just in time to

_____ the patient who was having a heart attack.

7. The cabin had insufficient **pressure** (               ) so the engineer had to

_____ it before take-off.

8. The fair ride accelerates **fast** (               ), so the operator reminded the

passengers to _____ their safety belts.

PHOTOCOPIABLE     ■SCHOLASTIC
www.scholastic.co.uk

# Verb prefixes

## Objective

To use verb prefixes to transform verbs into other verbs with different meanings.

## Background knowledge

Prefixes are specific letter groupings placed at the beginning of words to change them into other words. The base words can be nouns, adjectives, adverbs or verbs. The children focus specifically on verb prefixes that create or change the meaning of verbs. Unlike derivational suffixes, prefixes usually do not change the base word class, for example, *align – misalign*, *do – redo*. To help children understand the role of each prefix in relation to its meaning, write these verbs on the board and explore which prefix belongs with which root verb and how it alters meaning: *do*, *like*, *excite*, *centralise* and *behave*. Note that many verbs taking 'de' or 'dis' can also take 're' as a prefix. Occasionally more than one prefix can create the same meaning, for example *trust*: *mistrust* or *distrust*.

- 'dis' – opposite of, not
- 'de' – reverse action, get rid of
- 'mis' – wrong, opposite or lack of
- 'out' – exceeding, external
- 'un' – not
- 'fore' – before, in front of
- 'over' – over the limit
- 'inter' – between, among
- 're' – do again, back
- 'trans' – across, beyond
- 'pre – before, prior to
- 'under' – insufficiently
- 'sub' – under, secondary

## Activities

- **Photocopiable page 32 'Branch out'**
Children are given root verbs and tables containing prefixes to which they can add the root verbs to create new verbs. Encourage the children to say each new verb aloud to internalise its sound. Encourage the use of dictionaries to check that the words they have

created are real verbs and then to compare them to the meanings of the root verbs.
- **Photocopiable page 33 'Prefix partners'**
The children read the list of root verbs on the photocopiable sheet, saying each aloud with the different prefixes to find the correct partner. If a real verb is created, they add it to the correct box. As some root verbs can be affixed to more than one prefix (*appear*, *reappear*, *disappear*), verbs can go in more than one box. The children do not have to find all the possibilities. Encourage use of a dictionary to check the words to reinforce their knowledge of spelling and help them understand how prefixes can change a verb's meaning.
- **Photocopiable page 34 'Pick the prefix'**
Since some base verbs affix to more than one prefix, the children practise using context to choose the correct prefix. They read the sentences and choose the correct prefix to create sense. Occasionally, the meaning of a verb stays the same with more than one prefix (*mistrust – distrust*), in which case the children can choose.

## Further ideas

- **Spot the prefix:** Make a chart with verb prefixes ('mis', 'de', 'dis', 're', 'over') along one axis. Encourage the children to add verbs containing these prefixes to the chart as they encounter them. Remind them to check the verb is not a homograph by looking at the word in context (*recover*, *re-cover*).
- **Prefix possibilities:** Each day, introduce another prefix that can transform verbs: 'out', 'be', 'fore', 'un', 'inter', 'pre', 'sub', 'trans', 'under'. Challenge the children to notice verbs with these prefixes, write them on card together with the meaning and then pin them on a display area.

## Digital content

On the digital component you will find:
- Printable versions of all three photocopiable pages.
- Answers to all three photocopiable pages.
- Interactive versions of 'Branch out' and 'Pick the prefix'.

Name:

**Verb prefixes**

# Branch out

■ Create new verbs by combining the prefixes in the tables with the root verbs in the box below.

■ Write your new verbs in the tables. Use your dictionary to check the words you have made.

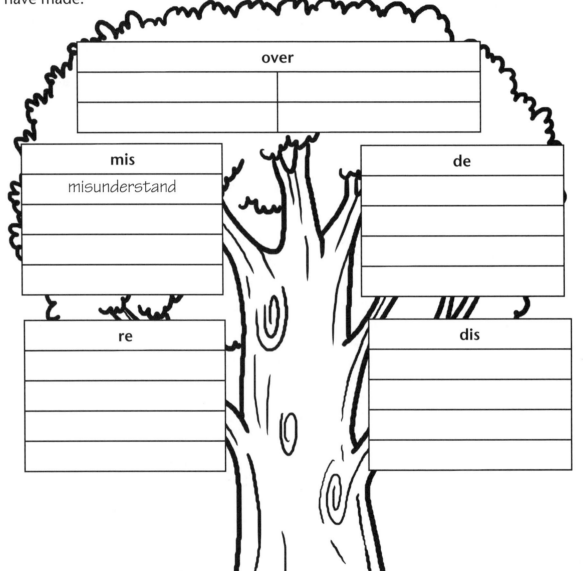

| over | |
|---|---|
| | |
| | |

| mis |
|---|
| misunderstand |
| |
| |
| |

| de |
|---|
| |
| |
| |

| re |
|---|
| |
| |
| |
| |

| dis |
|---|
| |
| |
| |

| Root verbs |
|---|
| understand   settle   able   see   build   hearten   mystify   grade   lead   classify |
| take   agree   colour   come   ride   view   rate   hydrate   behave   make |

## Verb prefixes

# Prefix partners

Each of these base verbs can be changed into a new verb by adding one or more of the prefixes from the boxes below.

■  Write any new verbs you make into the correct prefix box.

■  On a separate piece of paper, write a sentence for at least two of the new verbs from each prefix box, such as: *His mother warned him not to overdo it at football training.*

| | |
|---|---|
| use | **over** |
| appear | |
| grow | **dis** |
| construct | |
| generate | **de** |
| do | |
| connect | |
| value | **mis** |
| pay | |
| place | **re** |
| take | |
| solve | |
| trust | |

Name:

## Verb prefixes

# Pick the prefix

■ Choose the correct prefix from the box to add to the verb to make sense of each sentence.

■ Use a dictionary to check your choice if you are unsure.

| dis | re | over | de | mis |

1. Margie tried to _____solve sand in water but it didn't work.

2. Mr Grimm told me to _____write my homework because it was illegible.

3. Rianna broke the car window so her mum had to _____place it.

4. The motorcycle tried to _____take the car before the lights turned red.

5. The teacher had to _____connect the electricity for safety before reconnecting the wires.

6. I _____placed my key and had to knock on my neighbour's door to ask for the spare one.

7. Alan wished for a cloak to make him _____appear so he could sneak out from detention.

8. Mrs Davids is going to _____tire at the end of the year so we are going to hold a surprise party for her.

9. I am so _____organised that I cannot even find where I put my shoes.

10. The dogs had had nothing to drink so they were _____hydrated.

**PHOTOCOPIABLE**

**■ SCHOLASTIC**
www.scholastic.co.uk

# The hyphen

## Objective

To understand the purpose of the hyphen and to begin to use it in spelling.

## Background knowledge

A hyphen is a punctuation mark (-) primarily used to link words or separate syllables in a word. Commonly, hyphens create compound adjectives (*short-term*), nouns (*mother-in-law*) or verbs (*ice-skate*). In English, two words may initially be joined by a hyphen (*note-book*) but over time become a closed word (*notebook*). This lack of consistency in spelling with hyphens makes it confusing for the children. This section builds on previous work on verb prefixes by introducing prefixed verbs that may or may not be hyphenated. Hyphens can be used between prefixes and root words, for example, to avoid a double vowel (*co-operate*, *re-enter*), especially to clarify whether adjacent vowels are pronounced separately or merged as a diphthong (*deice* or *de-ice*). Note that this is not a clear rule – both *cooperate* and *co-operate* are acceptable, for example. The second compelling reason for using a hyphen in prefixed verbs is for clarification when adding the prefix creates a pre-existing word; for example, *resign* and *re-sign*.

## Activities

● **Photocopiable page 36 'Hyphenate to say it'**
At first glance, some words can be challenging to pronounce or understand using standard word attack skills, especially when prefixes ending in vowels are affixed to verbs beginning in vowels. The children will be familiar with graphemes 'ee', 'oo', 'ea' or 'ei', so show how the hyphen indicates a syllable split after the prefix. Get them to underline any prefixes they know before starting the activity: 're', 'de', 'mis', 'pre' (before) and 'co' (with) and discuss their meanings. As the words become familiar, the hyphen becomes less important and can often be dropped.

● **Photocopiable page 37 'Which is which?'**
A hyphen can also clarify the meaning of a word, for example, if a pre-existing homograph is created when a prefix is added to a verb. The children have to differentiate between the meaning of each word with and without a hyphen. Encourage them to use a dictionary to look up the word without the hyphen and compare it to the base verb to help them understand how the hyphen clarifies meaning.
● **Photocopiable page 38 'Which one?'**
These activities will help consolidate children's knowledge of prefixed verbs with and without hyphens. Remind the children that the hyphen is often optional but also remind them that the hyphen splitting the vowels into two syllables helps both pronunciation and understanding. Put these words on the board and discuss the meaning of each to revise how adding a prefix to a verb can cause confusion with a pre-existing word: *sent – resent – re-sent*.

## Further ideas

● **With or without:** Make a list of common verbs that can be written with or without hyphens (*co-operate*, *co-ordinate*, *mis-spell* and so on). Put both spellings side by side and run a tally chart underneath each time they notice the word. This will help them become familiar with both alternatives.
● **Verb, noun or adjective:** Sensitise the children to other uses of hyphens, by pointing it out each time you come across one in reading or general work. Encourage children to identify the word class (or whether it is a fraction or number-related word). Discuss why they think the hyphen may have been used: compound word, number for clarification and so on.

## Digital content

On the digital component you will find:
● Printable versions of all three photocopiable pages.
● Answers to 'Hyphenate to say it' and 'Which one?'.
● Interactive versions of 'Hyphenate to say it' and 'Which one?'.

Name:

# The hyphen

# Hyphenate to say it

Some verbs can be spelled with or without a hyphen between the prefix and the root verb. Hyphens are useful for showing you how to pronounce or make sense of a word, for example, *coop* (**oo** sounds like b**oo**t) or *co-op* (two sounds: long **o** followed by short **o**).

■   Say each verb aloud and then rewrite each one showing where you would use a hyphen to show how to pronounce it properly or make sense of it.

| | | |
|---|---|---|
| **reenact** | **deice** | **coown** |
| **prearrange** | **reselect** | **deemphasise** |
| **realign** | **missay** | **reask** |
| **cooperate** | **misspell** | **reissue** |
| **reexamine** | **reenter** | **reenergise** |
| **coordinate** | **missell** | **reignite** |

■   Choose four of the verbs and write a sentence using each of them on a separate piece of paper.

**PHOTOCOPIABLE**   ■SCHOLASTIC
                                                www.scholastic.co.uk

## The hyphen

# Which is which?

Sometimes, adding a prefix to a verb creates an existing word with the same spelling but a different meaning. A hyphen can be used in these situations to clarify the meaning.

■ Read each pair of words aloud and then write a sentence for each word to show the difference in meaning. The first pair has been done for you.

**resign:** *The teacher decided to resign from her job after she won the lottery.*
**re-sign:** *Mr Walters had to re-sign all the reports after spilling coffee over his signature.*

**recover:** _____

**re-cover:** _____

**react:** _____

**re-act:** _____

**reform:** _____

**re-form:** _____

**resent:** _____

**re-sent:** _____

**repress:** _____

**re-press:** _____

Name:

# The hyphen

# Which one?

■ Choose the correct prefix to add to each root verb to complete the passage. Use a hyphen between the prefix and the verb.

| re | co | mis | cross |
|---|---|---|---|

Kieran tried to begin his project on Ancient Mesopotamia for the school History

competition but _____spelled the key words in his Internet search. He was about

to _____search the Internet by _____entering the key words, spelled correctly this

time after consulting his dictionary, when the teacher _____ordinating the project

began to _____examine him on why he hadn't yet started his work.

■ Choose the correct verb to write in each space to make sense of the passage.

| recover | re-cover | reuse | reserved |
|---|---|---|---|
| re-heated | re-served | coordinate | |

Marlene decided to _____ her school books and to colour

_____ them according to subject. She tried to _____

her original labels, but it took so long that she missed lunch. The kitchen staff had

only just _____ her food after it had been _____,

when the bell rang. She then dashed to class and slipped into the place her friend

had _____, with barely time to _____ her breath.

# Assessment

## Assessment grid

The following grid shows the main objectives and activities covered in this chapter. You can use the grid to locate activities that cover a particular focus that you are keen to monitor.

| Objectives | Page | Activity title |
|---|---|---|
| To convert nouns or adjectives into verbs using suffixes. | 28 | Action suffixes |
| | 29 | Pot luck |
| | 30 | Make me a verb |
| To use verb prefixes. | 32 | Branch out |
| | 33 | Prefix partners |
| | 34 | Pick the prefix |
| To use hyphens to avoid ambiguity. | 36 | Hyphenate to say it |
| | 37 | Which is which? |
| | 38 | Which one? |

## Observation and record keeping

Exploring how the root word changes when the suffixes 'ate', 'ify' 'ise' and 'en' are added helps children connect their knowledge of nouns and adjectives with the resulting verbs and their spelling. Applying this knowledge provides children with patterns on which to base their spelling and understanding of tricky-sounding words. The skills needed to engage with these etymological activities are good for observation. Although hyphens are useful for linking prefixes to verbs to clarify punctuation and meaning, beware of children using hyphens by default and note those who do not recognise the prefix and attempt to pronounce the first part of the prefixed verb as one sound rather than syllabifying the prefix.

## Assessment activity

- **What you need**

A copy of photocopiable page 40 'Supercharged suffixes and prefixes' for each child, writing materials.

- **What to do**

Remind the children how some suffixes have the power to change nouns and adjectives into verbs. Ask the children for examples of both. Explain that the photocopiable sheet has three sections and to leave the challenge until the end. Go through the example in the first part. Then move on to the second part, noting the changes to the spelling of the root word. The prefixes activity has no example so ask for a volunteer to suggest which prefixes would go with the first verb in the list.

## Differentiation

- Work in small groups or orally with less confident learners, especially as these activities assess the children's understanding of word class as well as spelling skills. Allow them to leave out the challenge.
- Get more confident learners to complete the challenge box and ask them to explain how the words changed or did not follow a spelling rule when the suffix was added.

## Further learning

- **Etymology:** Use words found in other subjects as the basis for further research into etymology, especially words with prefixes. For example, *deci* means one tenth, so what does *decimate* mean?
- **Dictionary:** Encourage the children to use dictionaries fully, especially to check the spelling of suffixed and prefixed words.

Name:

## Assessment

# Supercharged suffixes and prefixes

■ Sort these words into the correct boxes.

| sympathy<br>strength<br>beauty<br>false<br>calibre<br>private | **Nouns:**<br>sympathy |
| --- | --- |
| | **Adjectives:** |

■ Add the correct suffix to turn each word into a verb and underline the suffix.
**Tip:** Remember the spelling rules for adding suffixes beginning with vowels.

| ise | ate | ify | en |
| --- | --- | --- | --- |

sympath<u>ise</u>     _____     _____

_____     _____     _____

■ Draw lines to match each base verb to one or more prefixes.

| pre | review | pre |
| --- | --- | --- |
| re | calculate | re |
| mis | mount | mis |
| | read | |
| dis | heat | dis |
| | place | |
| de | connect | de |
| | activate | |

■ **Challenge:** Turn these words into verbs by adding a suffix. Check your spelling in a dictionary:

different _____ ☐          horror _____ ☐

identity _____ ☐          analysis _____ ☐

# Chapter 3

# Word endings

## Introduction

Word endings, particularly those that sound familiar, can be tricky to get right. Syllabification and correct pronunciation will help the children to sound out the word and identify the final syllable. Knowing some helpful rules (and the exceptions) will give the children confidence to work out the word endings and then apply them to words so that they become familiar with them. Let them use the Look, Say, Cover, Write, Check approach to practise the correct word endings, making sure they are aware of the root word and other words in the word family. Having fun with the words will add positively to the learning experience so, where possible, play word games that will help commit the words to memory. For further practice, please see the 'Word endings' section in the Year 5 workbook.

## In this chapter

| | |
|---|---|
| **Which ending?** page 43 | To spell words ending in 'cious' or 'tious'. |
| **Rules and exceptions** page 47 | To spell words ending in 'cial' or 'tial'. |
| **Tricky letter strings** page 51 | To spell words ending in 'ant'/'ance'/'ancy' and 'ent'/ 'ence'/'ency', making appropriate choices. |
| **Assessment** page 55 | Activities and ideas to assess use of word endings. |

## Poster notes

### Word endings (page 42)
The poster page is a useful reference for the children when completing the activities and revising the work. Ensure that the children use the correct pronunciation when sounding out the different word endings. They should understand the rules to apply them. Ask them to give other examples to add to the ones already provided. The exceptions must be committed to memory so let them make up word games, rhymes, songs or raps to aid with this.

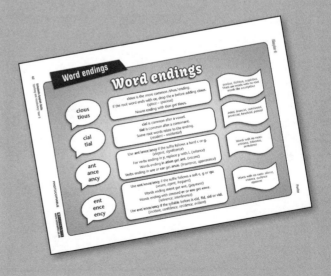

# Word endings

## Word endings

**cious** is the more common /**shus**/ ending.

If the root word ends with **ce**, drop the **e** before adding **cious**. (space – spacious)

Nouns ending with **tion** get **tious**.

*anxious, fictitious, suspicious. There are words with no root words like scrumptious*

---

**cial** is common after a vowel.

**tial** is common after a consonant.

Some root words relate to the ending. (resident – residential)

*initial, financial, commercial, provincial, beneficial, palatial*

---

Use **ant/ance/ancy** if the suffix follows a hard **c** or **g**. (elegant, significance)

For verbs ending in **y**, replace **y** with **i**. (reliance)

Words ending in **ation** get **ant**. (vacant)

Verbs ending in **ure** or **ear** get **ance**. (insurance, appearance)

*Words with no roots: entrance, tolerance, ambulance*

---

Use **ent/ence/ency** if the suffix follows a soft **c**, **g** or **qu**. (recent, agent, frequent)

Words ending **ment** get **ent**. (payment)

Words ending with stressed **er** or **ere** get **ence**. (reference, interference)

Use **ent/ence/ency** if the syllable before is **cid**, **fid**, **sid** or **vid**. (incident, confidence, residence, evident)

*Words with no roots: silence, violence, audience apparent*

---

cious
tious

cial
tial

ant
ance
ancy

ent
ence
ency

**PHOTOCOPIABLE**

SCHOLASTIC
www.scholastic.co.uk

# Which ending?

## Objective

To spell words ending in 'cious' or 'tious'.

## Background knowledge

This section deals with word endings that have not yet been covered in the curriculum. The children are now familiar with the idea that a word ending usually changes the form and/or function of a word. In this section they learn that the word endings 'cious' and 'tious' have Latin origins, meaning 'full of' or 'having' and usually indicate an adjective (*she is gracious – full of grace*). The /sh/ sound is made either using 'ti' or 'ci'. Most word endings that sound like /shus/ are spelled 'cious' and this is clear from the root word. If the root word ends 'ce', the 'e' is dropped and 'ious' is added to form the adjective (*office – officious*). Root words ending with a /shun/ sound become adjectives ending with 'tious' (*ambition – ambitious*). Exceptions to this are *fiction – fictitious* and *suspicion – suspicious*. Some words have no root word and so they must simply be learned (*facetious, scrumptious* and *surreptitious*).

## Activities

● **Photocopiable page 44 'Meet the /shus/ friends'**
Although this introduces the children to both word endings 'cious' and 'tious', the activity focuses on the 'cious' ending. Ask the children why they think the sounds are introduced as friends. The letters in these word endings always stick together (like friends) and both endings sound similar. Spelling requires visual recognition and some learners benefit from picturing the sounds as 'friends'. Read examples of words ending with the /shus/ sound and discuss the word class to which they belong. Ask what clue they can find in the root word ('ce') to help them remember to add 'cious'.
● **Photocopiable page 45 'Describe it with tious'**
Words ending in 'tious' are mostly adjectives. There is a lot of difficult vocabulary here and the children should learn to use the words in the correct context. Ask them

to identify and underline what or who is being described in each sentence. They will need to learn the words that are exceptions. Use this opportunity to highlight the difference in meaning and pronunciation of *conscious, conscience* and *conscientious*.
● **Photocopiable page 46 '/Shus/ the correct ending'**
On this photocopiable page, the children revise the words and ensure they are familiar with 'cious' and 'tious' word endings and when to use them. Revise the rules by asking a volunteer to explain it to the class. You can also get the children to work in pairs, taking turns to explain the rules to each other and also test each other.

## Further ideas

● **Chopped!:** Give the children a list of all the words covered in this section and ask them to show where they would 'chop' off the word ending of each word. Use the board and do it as a class, or let them sit in groups and work on paper or mini boards.
● **Guess it right:** The children take turns to stand in front of the class and describe a 'cious' or 'tious' word without using the word or any root word. The others must try to guess which word it is.
● **Dictionary dash:** Make sure everyone has a dictionary, or let them work in pairs and share. Call out a word and see who is first to find the word in a dictionary. The first person to find the word and place their finger on it must shout 'got it'. This person gets to call the next word.

## Digital content

On the digital component you will find:
● Printable versions of all three photocopiable pages.
● Answers to all three photocopiable pages.
● Interactive versions of 'Meet the /shus/ friends' and '/shus/ the correct ending'.

Name:

## Which ending?

# Meet the /shus/ friends

They're word endings that sound exactly the same and their letters always stick together. They like to change words into adjectives. Your challenge is to work out which /**shus**/ you need for a particular word.

| cious |  | tious |

■  Most /**shus**/ endings are spelled **cious**. Change these nouns to adjectives by replacing the **ce** at the end of the word with **cious**. Write the new word next to the matching synonym. The first one has been done for you.

**Nouns**

office
space
vice
grace
malice
auspice
avarice

cious

**Adjectives**

|          | cruel      |
|----------|------------|
|          | greedy     |
| officious | interfering |
|          | favourable |
|          | elegant    |
|          | roomy      |
|          | dangerous  |

■  Shake on it. These word beginnings end with a vowel. Join **cious** to each word beginning to complete the words. One has been done.

suspi
atro
auda
deli

cious

fero
tena
capa
vora

cious

| suspicious |  |  |
|------------|--|--|
|            |  |  |
|            |  |  |

# Which ending?

# Describe it with tious

■ Let **tious** help you change these nouns into adjectives. Circle the words in each clue that end with **tion** and replace it with **tious**.

A businessman full of ambition.

| | | | t | i | o | u | s | |

A child that walks with caution.

| | | t | i | o | u | s | |

A discussion filled with contention.

| | | | | t | i | o | u | s |

A speedy, successful expedition.

| | | | | t | i | o | u | s |

A sick person with an infection.

| | | | t | i | o | u | s |

A healthy meal with vitamins and nutrition.

| | | | t | i | o | u | s |

A person who puts on a front and is full of pretention.

| | | | t | i | o | u | s |

The repetition of work before exams.

| | | | t | i | o | u | s |

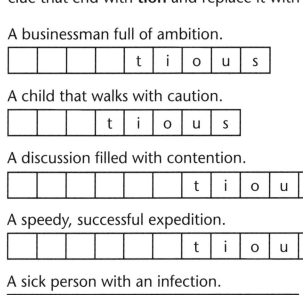

■ These adjectives don't come from a noun – you just have to get to know them. Add **tious** to complete each word.

Someone who works very hard is

| c | o | n | s | c | i | e | n | | | | | | |

A rude person is

| f | a | c | e | | | | | |

A tasty meal is

| s | c | r | u | m | p | | | | | |

A secretive person is

| s | u | r | r | e | p | t | i | | | | | |

Name:

## Which ending?

# /shus/ the correct ending

■ Pick a word from the box. Use the key to work out which words get which ending. Beware! Words in **bold** are exceptions!

avarice    malice    audacity    ambition

**conscience**    auspice    **suspicion**

repetition    capacity    ferocity    infection

caution    atrocity    tenacity    **fiction**

Does it end with **ce** or **city**?

cious me!

tious me!

Does it end with **tion**?

■ Use these adjectives to describe the following.

1. Someone who works hard and strives to do well. _____

2. A person who thinks about money all the time. _____

3. A story that is made up. _____

4. An instruction that is given over and over. _____

5. An important and happy occasion. _____

6. Someone who does horrible things to others. _____

7. To be very careful. _____

8. Someone who does not trust others. _____

9. A very dangerous animal. _____

10. Someone who sticks to a task no matter the cost. _____

# Rules and exceptions

To spell words ending in 'cial' or 'tial'.

## Background knowledge

These word endings are pronounced /shul/ and are used to form adjectives describing the quality of something. The rule is a simple one but remind the children that there are exceptions. The 'cial' ending is commonly used after a vowel and the 'tial' after a consonant letter. Make sure that everyone knows their vowels and consonants. However, in some cases this rule does not apply and these exceptions are covered in the activities to help the children become familiar with them. In some exceptions, the spelling is related to the root word. The root word *finance*, with 'ce', becomes *financial* with 'cial', *commerce* becomes *commercial* and *province* becomes *provincial*. Other exceptions are the words *initial*, ending with 'tial' after a vowel and *palatial*, also ending with 'tial' after the vowel. Many root words ending with 't' take the 'tial' ending, but not always, as in the word *benefit* – *beneficial*.

## Activities

● **Photocopiable page 48 'Which one cial/tial it be?'**
This photocopiable sheet gives the children an opportunity to discover the rule for themselves. Begin by writing the word beginnings on the board. Ask the children to find the common element. If they are unable to come up with an answer, circle the final letter of each word beginning and ask them to look again. Once they have discussed these observations, they will be ready to formulate and apply a rule.

● **Photocopiable page 49 'News flash: Exceptions in hiding'**
The rule for using 'cial' or 'tial' is not always reliable. This photocopiable sheet will give the children a chance to become familiar with words that don't follow the rule. Let them begin by looking for the words in the word search. They should look for the letter strings 'cial' and 'tial' and this will lead them to the word beginnings. Ask the children to explain why these words are exceptions – can they identify how these words don't follow the rule.

● **Photocopiable page 50 'Rap it up'**
This photocopiable sheet revises the word endings covered so far in this chapter. The children should complete the rap using the correct word endings. If time permits encourage them to add to the rap. Let them make up their own rap using other word endings covered in the chapter. In small groups they can share and perform other raps. To shorten this activity, they can make up a short rhyme or pair up words that go together.

## Further ideas

● **Make a dash:** Move the children into a large space and sort them into small groups. Place two containers in the centre of the space each labelled 'cial' and 'tial'. Call out a word, let them write down the word and their group number, then one person should run and place the word into the correct container. At the end, count the correct answers and give a score to each group.

● **Roll the dice:** Organise the children into groups of six. Each group needs a dice and a small set of cards with different word endings written on each card (*cial*, *tial*, *cious*, *tious*). Allocate a number (1–6) to each person in the group. Throw the dice to see who begins. The first player picks up a card, reads the word ending and comes up with a word for this word ending. This person then throws the dice and the next player has a turn.

## Digital content

On the digital component you will find:
● Printable versions of all three photocopiable pages.
● Answers to all three photocopiable pages.
● Interactive version of 'Which one cial/tial it be?'.

Name:

# Which one cial/tial it be?

The word endings **cial** and **tial** (pronounced /**shul**/) mean 'having the quality of'. They make adjectives.

■ Add **cial** to these word beginnings.

offi_____        sacrifi_____        artifi_____

What do you notice about the letter at the end of these word beginnings?

_____

■ Add **tial** to these word beginnings.

par_____        confiden_____        essen_____

What do you notice about the letter at the end of these word beginnings?

_____

■ Make up a rule for using **cial** or **tial** as a word ending.

My rule: _____

■ Now use this rule to decide if these words end with **cial** or **tial**. Write them next to the correct word meaning.

| Word beginning | | Meaning |
|---|---|---|
| par | _____ | A large, noisy downpour |
| mar | _____ | In number order |
| so | _____ | Warlike |
| residen | _____ | Living together with others |
| judi | _____ | A living space |
| poten | _____ | A large, significant amount |
| cru | _____ | To be fair and objective |
| substan | _____ | Part of or unfair |
| torren | _____ | Conducted by a court |
| sequen | _____ | Having the ability to achieve |
| impar | _____ | Something very important |

**PHOTOCOPIABLE**   SCHOLASTIC
www.scholastic.co.uk

**Rules and exceptions**

# News flash: Exceptions in hiding

It has been reported that some /**shul**/ word endings have bent the rules again and have gone into hiding. Law enforcement officers have been sent to investigate their whereabouts. Witnesses say they saw them disappear into a crowd of letters.

■  Help the law enforcement officers find six /**shul**/ words in this word search that have not followed the rule.

■  Write the words you find on the lines below.

**Tip:** Look for the letter strings **cial** and **tial**.

| l | a | i | c | n | i | v | o | r | p | z | c |
|---|---|---|---|---|---|---|---|---|---|---|---|
| g | r | e | b | h | y | l | j | l | d | o | l |
| l | m | v | o | b | p | g | a | d | m | w | a |
| u | a | b | v | r | x | i | m | m | k | p | i |
| l | x | i | k | e | t | d | e | w | q | l | c |
| u | u | j | c | a | u | r | i | s | f | t | n |
| e | e | z | l | i | c | f | v | q | x | s | a |
| n | x | a | d | i | f | g | q | x | k | x | n |
| r | p | u | a | x | h | e | d | a | r | r | i |
| c | c | l | x | u | k | e | n | s | r | d | f |
| i | n | i | t | i | a | l | c | e | a | v | w |
| s | v | m | u | k | q | m | p | u | b | f | y |

_____     _____

_____     _____

_____     _____

■  Look these words up in a dictionary and then use them to write sentences of your own on the back of this page.

Name:

# Rap it up

■ Use the /shul/ words you have learned to complete this rap about the importance of using correct spelling in written work.

This message is hardly confiden_____.

To tell everyone is preferen_____:

Proper spelling is benefi_____,

So pay attention because it's essen_____

To anything commer_____, or judi_____;

To all things offi_____

And places provin_____.

You may be feeling impar_____

And think this stuff is superfi_____,

But with all that spelling poten_____

Watch out! Keep writing free of errors substan_____

Avoid silly mistakes – this is cru_____!

I'll say it once more – good spelling is influen_____.

■ Now, use word endings **cious** and **tious** to make up a rap about friendship. Here are two lines to get you started. Complete the rest on the back of this page.

<u>Friendship</u>

From real life stories and books fictitious,
It's clear that friendship is infectious.

PHOTOCOPIABLE

# Tricky letter strings

## Objective

To spell words ending in 'ant'/'ance'/'ancy' and 'ent'/'ence'/'ency', making appropriate choices.

## Background knowledge

A large number of words are difficult to spell because of slight subtleties in the vowel choice at the end of the word. Use 'ent' and 'ence'/'ency' after a soft 'c' (/s/ sound), soft 'g' (/j/ sound) and 'qu', or if there is a related word with a clear short /e/ sound in the right position. Use 'ant' and 'ance'/'ancy' if there is a related word with a short /a/ or /ai/ sound in the right position; 'ation' endings are often a clue. There are many words, however, where these rules don't apply and other methods must be applied. Use a combination of breaking the word into syllables (exaggerating the pronunciation of each one – *am-bu-lance*), using visual strategies (does the word look right?) and mnemonics to develop spelling knowledge and strategies. It is also helpful to look at the other words in the word family as this may provide some helpful spelling clues.

## Activities

● **Photocopiable page 52 'ant or ent?'**
Words containing the suffixes 'ant' or 'ent' are often tricky to spell. The suffix 'ant' means being in a particular condition such as 'dependant'. The suffix 'ent', on the other hand means someone that performs a particular action, for example, 'agent'. By understanding the meaning of each suffix, the children will be assisted in choosing which suffix is correct.
● **Photocopiable page 53 'ance or ence?'**
In this activity, the children work out their own rules based on the lists of words provided. Try not to refer to the poster page at this point until they have made an attempt to work it out themselves. The final task deals with words that don't have a rule – the tricky endings have been provided. Ask the children to think of a way to remember each of the words; they may find breaking

it up into syllables helps or they may prefer to use memory and visual checks.
● **Photocopiable page 54 'Relationships'**
In this activity, the children do three short activities to explore the relationship between words that change from 'ant' to 'ance'/'ancy' and from 'ent' to 'ence'/'ency' and vice versa. As they work through the activities, encourage them to say the sentences aloud and over-pronounce the 'e' or 'a' sounds. After completing the activities, encourage them to invent mnemonics to remind them whether the word uses 'ant', 'ance', 'ent' or 'ence' (for example: *I see a distant ant*).

## Further ideas

● **Post boxes:** Provide labelled pairs of post boxes ('ance'/'ancy' and 'ence'/'ency') in an interactive spelling area in the class. Next to the boxes place picture prompt cards with writing spaces beneath each. Children write the spelling beneath the picture and post the cards in the correct boxes. At the end of the week empty out the post boxes and check the spellings as a class.
● **Word a day:** Challenge the children to use a word a day from each of the activities in their own writing. Each time one of the target words is used, let them highlight the word and give themselves a star or a smiley face in their book.
● **Spelling journals:** As the children encounter other words with the same letter strings in their personal reading, encourage them to add them to their spelling journals.

## Digital content

On the digital component you will find:
● Printable versions of all three photocopiable pages.
● Answers to all three photocopiable pages.
● Interactive version of 'ant or ent?'.

Name:

## Tricky letter strings

# ant or ent?

**Tip:** The word endings **ant** and **ent** mean *one who is*. Generally, **ant** is about being and **ent** is about doing.

■ Read the definition. Is it about one who is *being* or one who is *doing*? Choose the correct word ending. Write the word in the correct box.

■ Check your word in a dictionary and fill in the word class.

| Definition | Word beginning | Ending: ant/ent? | Word class |
|---|---|---|---|
| A person who acts as a go-between | ag | | |
| Not keen to do something | reluct | | |
| Slow to act due to lack of confidence | hesit | | |
| Somebody who replies to a letter | respond | | |
| Relying on somebody or something for help | depend | | |
| Someone who is supported financially | depend | | |
| Able to act on their own without help from others | independ | | |
| Lit by a bright or glowing light | radi | | |
| Somebody who has a law case brought against them | defend | | |
| Doing something of very good quality | excell | | |
| Being up to date | relev | | |
| One who sends letters to another person | correspond | | |
| Doing something often | frequ | | |
| An empty space | vac | | |

## Tricky letter strings

# ance or ence?

■ Add the word ending **ance** or **ancy** to each of these words. Write the new words underneath the original words.

| apply | domination | assure | appear |
| rely | hesitation | insure | forbear |
| ally | expectation | endure | clear |

My rule: _____

■ Complete these words using the word ending **ence** or **ency**.

| intellig_____ | confid_____ | adher_____ | refer_____ |
| consqu_____ | resid_____ | interfere_____ | prefer_____ |
| innoc_____ | coincid_____ | | confer_____ |
| | evid_____ | | |

My rule: _____

■ Some words don't go by the rules – you just have to learn them. Use a dictionary to complete the word puzzles using the correct ending.

A proficient expert displays this quality.

| | | | | | | e | n | c | y |

A door or gate through which people enter.

| | | | | a | n | c | e |

A group of people watching a show.

| | | | | e | n | c | e |

The use of physical force to hurt someone.

| | | | | e | n | c | e |

A period during which someone is not present.

| | | | | e | n | c | e |

A vehicle used to take people to hospital.

| | | | | a | n | c | e |

Name:

# Tricky letter strings

# Relationships

Words endings **ant/ance/ancy**, and **ent/ence/ency** usually make nouns or adjectives.

■   Write the adjective or the noun that is missing from these sentences. Use the word in bold to help you. The first one has been done for you.

**Tip:** Remember to use the last letters in the words as clues to help you choose the correct word ending. Then check your spelling in a dictionary.

1. In the **distance** I could see a *distant* tower.

2. He proved his **innocence** and walked away as an _____ man.

3. The **intelligent** boy worked hard to show his _____.

4. An **elegant** woman walks with grace and _____.

5. The **disobedient** dog was taken to _____ classes.

6. The **hesitant** builder had to explain his _____.

7. It is common _____ to behave in a **decent** manner.

8. When he saw a _____ he filled the **vacant** spot.

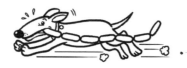

■   Change these adjectives into nouns.

relevant _____

evident _____

important _____

ignorant _____

absent _____

correspondent _____

hesitant _____

frequent _____

■   Change these nouns into adjectives.

violence _____

abundance _____

fragrance _____

difference _____

convenience _____

excellence _____

vacancy _____

decency_____

# Assessment

## Assessment grid

The following grid shows the main objectives and activities covered in this chapter. You can use the grid to locate activities that cover a particular focus that you are keen to monitor.

| Objective | Page | Activity title |
|---|---|---|
| To use and spell endings 'cial' and 'tial' and 'cious' and 'tious'. | 44 | Meet the /shus/ friends |
| | 45 | Describe it with tious |
| | 46 | /shus/ the correct ending |
| | 48 | Which one cial/tial it be? |
| | 49 | News flash: Exceptions in hiding |
| | 50 | Rap it up |
| To use and spell words ending in 'ant', 'ance', 'ent', 'ence' and 'ency'. | 52 | ant or ent? |
| | 53 | ance or ence? |
| | 54 | Relationships |

## Observation and record keeping

While the children are carrying out independent writing tasks, circulate carrying a whiteboard and pen. Prompt them to visually check for errors. If the incorrect letter string has been chosen for a specific word, prompt the children to suggest other ways in which the sound can be represented – test out each one on your whiteboard and encourage the children to decode which they feel is correct. When marking across the curriculum, keep a check of particular spelling rules which are often broken – revisit these as a class when necessary.

## Assessment activity

● **What you need**
The table from photocopiable page 56 'Choosing correct endings' for each child, writing materials.
● **What to do**
The children must read the words in the first column and decide which word ending will change the word into an adjective. Once they are sure of the correct ending, they should write the word down in the second column. Once the activity has been marked and a score given, the children should be given time to do corrections. This gives them the opportunity to see and correct their errors. These words should be written down in the last column.

## Differentiation

● The list of words provided is divided into two parts. The first part has easier words with no exceptions. You can use this as an introduction or warm-up activity or to assess less confident learners.
● The second part has more difficult words and contains spelling exceptions. Use this as an extension activity or to assess more confident spellers.

## Further learning

● **Pair up:** Let the children sit in pairs and test each other using the words covered in this chapter.
● **Spell check:** Place the children in groups. Each group represents a different word ending. Call out a word. The relevant group must respond by calling out 'Spell check' and then receive a point. If a group responds incorrectly, they lose a point. This also works well if children are placed in pairs.

Name:

# Assessment

# Choosing correct endings

■ Read the noun in the first column. Make the word into an adjective by choosing the correct word ending.

| cial/tial | cious/tious | ant/ance/ancy | ent/ence/ency |

| Noun | Adjective | Corrections |
|------|-----------|-------------|
| confidence | | |
| caution | | |
| grace | | |
| relevance | | |
| sacrifice | | |
| resident | | |

■ You're doing well. Now try some more challenging words.

| | | |
|------|-----------|-------------|
| fiction | | |
| rely | | |
| absence | | |
| proficiency | | |
| palace | | |
| excellence | | |
| Score | | |

**PHOTOCOPIABLE**

■ SCHOLASTIC
www.scholastic.co.uk

# Chapter 4

# Word families, roots and origins

## Introduction

The chapter begins by deconstructing words into component elements to reinforce the children's understanding of and dexterity with morphology (a word's internal make-up in terms of root words, prefixes and suffixes). This knowledge is developed in the section on compound word formation and the plural form with its associated spelling rules, many of which also relate to word etymology (a word's history). The chapter progresses the children's knowledge of word families and the origins (Latin, Greek and French) of prefixes and root words. Decoding the discrete elements of complex words through etymology and morphology provides a strategy to help children to independently spell and understand many complex words. For further practice, please see the 'Word families, roots and origins' section in the Year 5 workbook.

## In this chapter

## Poster notes

**Where do words come from? (page 58)**
Invite volunteers to say each of the words at the top of the poster aloud and guess what they mean. Ask the children if they recognise any parts of the words from other words. Use the bottom part of the poster to demonstrate how some of the roots can be joined to several different prefixes and/or suffixes. Encourage the children to suggest words that can be built up from the different elements in the table. Invite a child to point out a spelling rule that they notice as the complex word builds up.

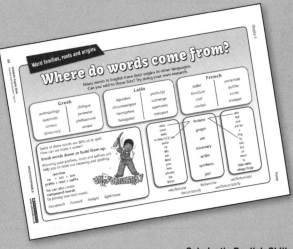

## Word families, roots and origins

# Where do words come from?

Many words in English have their origins in other languages.
Can you add to these lists? Try doing your own research.

### French

| | |
|---|---|
| ballet | parachute |
| brochure | quiche |
| chef | secret |
| crochet | trumpet |

### Greek

| | |
|---|---|
| anthropology | dialogue |
| automatic | perimeter |
| century | philharmonic |
| democracy | unique |

### Latin

| | |
|---|---|
| aqueduct | postscript |
| circumnavigate | submerge |
| hemisphere | supersonic |
| hexagonal | transport |

| | | |
|---|---|---|
| ate | | |
| ful | | |
| ure | | |
| ed/es | | |
| s | | |
| ing | | |
| ly | | |
| est | | |
| ise | | |
| al | | |
| ness | | |
| ic | | |
| ible/able | | |
| ology/logy | | |

fortune

graph

use

necessary

scribe

synthesis

ject

| |
|---|
| mis |
| over |
| anti |
| in/im/ir/il/un |
| auto |
| re |
| dis |
| en |
| deci |
| pre |
| bio |
| photo |
| de |
| inter |

mis/fortune

fortun/ate

fortun/ate/ly

un/fortun/ate

un/fortun/ate/ly

Some of these words are difficult to spell.
How can we make it easier?

**Break words down or build them up.**

Knowing your prefixes, roots and suffixes will
help you to work out meaning and spelling.

*reaction*
re  +  act  +  ion
prefix + root + suffix

We can also create
**compound words**
by joining two root words.

housework   firework   firelight   lighthouse

**PHOTOCOPIABLE**

■SCHOLASTIC
www.scholastic.co.uk

# Word structure

To use knowledge of word structure as an aid to spelling.

This section is about using knowledge of morphology in spelling. A root word is a word to which beginnings (prefixes) and endings (suffixes) can be added to create new words. Complex words may have both a prefix and a suffix, or even more than one suffix. Knowledge of root words, along with a growing knowledge of prefixes and suffixes, will assist in developing spelling strategies and building vocabulary. Adding a prefix rarely changes the spelling of a root word, but it can change the pronunciation; it is therefore important for the children to quickly be able to separate the prefix from the root word to identify the root. Suffixes, however, often change the spelling of a root word, especially if it ends in 'y', 'i', 'e' or a consonant preceded by a short vowel. Knowing the spelling rules associated with adding suffixes will assist the learners to spell complex words.

● **Photocopiable page 60 'Back to roots'**
Before starting the activity, write *comfort* on the board. Challenge pairs to find other words with the root word *comfort* within them (*comforts, comforted, comforting, discomfort, comfortable, uncomfortable, comfortably, uncomfortably, comforter*). Invite suggestions and record them on the board discussing how adding the prefixes and suffixes develops the meaning of the word. After the discussion, the children should work through the activity independently. Encourage the use of a dictionary.

● **Photocopiable page 61 'Word maths'**
Before doing the activity, talk about 'words sums' with the children and recap that prefixes and suffixes can change the meaning, class or tense of a root word. Use the word *friend* as a base for demonstrating how prefixes and suffixes progressively build more complex words. Point out that spelling rules apply even between

suffixes: *friend, friend + ly, friend + li + ness*. Write *fortune* on the board and invite volunteers to create word sums using it as the root: *misfortune, fortunate* (note the 'e' is dropped), *fortunately, unfortunately*.

● **Photocopiable page 62 'Root it out'**
Ask the children to list as many prefixes and suffixes as they can remember and write them under relevant headings on the board. Choose one of the root words and discuss which prefixes and/or suffixes could be added to it. This both revises previous work and prepares them for the words to find in the word search. Note that the word search contains diagonal and back-to-front words as well as up, down and across ones.

● **Challenge:** Choose other words to launch root word challenges as a regular warm-up activity, sometimes to add only suffixes or prefixes, but at other times for both. Consider making it a timed activity and then share the words each child or pair has found.

● **Add me up:** Make cards for regular suffixes and prefixes and put them into easy, more challenging or difficult packs containing root words to build more complex words.

● **Spot me:** Choose a prefix or suffix of the day or the week and encourage children to 'buzz' or put up their hand if they notice it in the course of the day's or the week's ordinary classes, especially in other subjects. Allow the child to add it to a running list on the wall, separating the word out into a word sum and underlining the relevant prefix or suffix of the day.

On the digital component you will find:
● Printable versions of all three photocopiable pages.
● Answers to all three photocopiable pages.
● Interactive versions of 'Back to roots' and 'Word maths'.

Name:

# Word structure

# Back to roots

■ Use red to underline the root word in each box. Use blue to underline prefixes that have been added to the root words. Use green to underline any suffixes added to the root words.

■ Watch out! Some root words may have both prefixes and suffixes!

development

developer

unequal

managing

equality

developmental

friendless

unemployed

redevelop

employee

unmanageable

overdeveloped

manager

friendship

equalise

unfriendly

friendly

equalisation

employer

inequality

friendliness

manageable

manages

equally

employed

unemployment

■ Group the words in the table below under the correct root word.

| employ | manage | develop | equal | friend |
|--------|--------|---------|-------|--------|
|        |        |         |       |        |
|        |        |         |       |        |
|        |        |         |       |        |
|        |        |         |       |        |
|        |        |         |       |        |
|        |        |         |       |        |

## Word structure

# Word maths

■ Complete the suffix, prefix and root word sums below and write the new word in the space provided. The first one has been done for you.

**Tip:** Remember to apply the spelling rules for adding suffixes!

love + ly =      *lovely* _____

interrupt + ion = _____

alien + ate = _____

re + act + ion = _____

enthral + ed = _____

happy + ness = _____

up + set + ing = _____

under + privilege + ed = _____

un + fortune + ate = _____

in + describe + able = _____

un + mis + take + able = _____

It's unmistakably him!

---

## Challenge

Create as many different words as you can by adding the prefixes and suffixes to the root word. Remember: root words can have both prefixes and suffixes, or even more than one of each. Check your words with a dictionary.

| **Root word: act** | **Prefixes and suffixes** |
|---|---|
| *active* | or |
| | re |
| | ive |
| | trans |
| | ion |
| | over |
| | un |
| | in |
| | ly |

**SCHOLASTIC**
www.scholastic.co.uk    **PHOTOCOPIABLE**          **Scholastic English Skills**
Spelling and vocabulary: Year 5    **61**

Name:

## Word structure

# Root it out

■ Circle as many words as you can find with these root words.

| honest | love | appoint | elect |

| d | y | o | l | o | v | i | n | g | u | i | n | n | e | y |
|---|---|---|---|---|---|---|---|---|---|---|---|---|---|---|
| i | l | y | a | o | n | v | p | k | h | v | d | l | l | w |
| s | t | h | c | e | v | t | e | a | y | i | e | t | b | n |
| a | s | d | e | b | d | e | i | f | s | c | s | y | t | v |
| p | e | e | z | j | s | m | l | h | t | e | l | p | g | y |
| p | n | t | e | a | p | p | o | i | n | t | m | e | n | t |
| o | o | n | l | l | b | n | v | o | n | u | z | t | y | s |
| i | h | i | e | z | e | e | h | q | u | e | j | s | l | e |
| n | e | o | c | s | y | s | g | k | d | e | s | k | e | n |
| t | l | p | t | n | i | o | p | p | a | e | r | s | v | o |
| u | e | p | i | d | l | t | c | e | l | e | e | r | o | h |
| w | c | a | o | o | l | o | v | e | a | b | l | e | l | s |
| a | t | s | n | d | b | j | v | b | e | l | o | v | e | d |
| l | o | i | v | q | f | o | d | e | t | c | e | l | e | v |
| g | r | d | v | o | l | e | j | i | r | y | j | i | g | a |

■ Write the words you have found in the columns below then use red to underline the root word.

🔍 *Which root word sometimes changes its spelling?*

| **honest** | **love** | **appoint** | **elect** |
|---|---|---|---|
| honest + ly | | | |
| | | | |
| | | | |
| | | | |
| | | | |
| | | | |
| | | | |

# Plurals and compound words

## Objective

To explore plural inflections and investigate the structure of compound words, using this knowledge to help spelling.

## Background knowledge

Some nouns are *countable* and others are *uncountable*. Countable nouns have a plural form, whereas uncountable nouns do not. The children will revise and practise some rules or patterns on how nouns turn into their plural form. New words are created in a number of ways: compounding (at least two root words in the morphology), blending (parts of two or more root words combine making a word that combines the meaning of both roots) and clipping (a shortened word whose meaning is unchanged from the original). This section focuses on compound words. Some compounds appear as two words, a single or hyphenated word – this may change over time. In other cases, the hyphen indicates that the words form a unit with a meaning separate to the words individually: *a light, blue chair* or *a light-blue chair*.

## Activities

● **Photocopiable page 64 'Adding s, es and ves'**
In this activity the children do word sums to practise plurals of words ending in 'sh', 'ch', 'x' and 'ss' adding 'es'. Note that some words ending in 'ch' with the /k/ sound only add 's'. The sheet also covers the plurals where words ending in 'f' or 'fe' drop it to add 'ves'. Note that there are exceptions to this rule, and some can be spelled either way: words ending in 'ff' just add 's'. Some words ending in 'o' just add 's'.
● **Photocopiable page 65 'Plural rules'**
Before they start the crossword, revise regular pluralisation rules on the board and discuss irregular plurals, such as *scissors*, *mice*. The answers to the crossword clues are plural nouns covering the various rules together with a few irregular plurals.

● **Photocopiable page 66 'Compound word battleships'**
For this two-player game, give each child a copy of the grid and a set of root words. Ask them to make five compound words by combining their root words and then to write them on the grid, vertically or horizontally. Once ready, they call out coordinates to each other. If the coordinate has a word on it, it is a hit: the letter and its root word must be called out. The attacker then has another turn to try to hit the conjoining root word. If they do, the defender says the root word. The attacker sinks the ship if they correctly guess the compound word. If they miss or guess wrongly, the other player has a turn. The winner is the first player to sink all their opponent's compound words.

## Further ideas

● **Perplexing plurals:** Challenge groups of children to create posters of nouns that have no singular (*scissors*), that are the same in the plural as in the singular (*sheep*), or that are irregular in the plural (*tooth – teeth*; *child – children*).
● **Plural challenge:** Divide the class into teams and give each team a set of pluralisation cards such as + 'es', drop 'y' + 'ies', + 's', drop 'f' + 'ves', and a joker (for exceptions). Prepare a list of nouns to call out or hold up. Each team displays the ending it thinks is correct, gaining a point for each correct answer – the first team to 20 points wins.
● **Bingo:** Challenge the children to make their own version of bingo with compound words. The caller could read out compound words and the other children could have the root words written on their cards.

## Digital content

On the digital component you will find:
● Printable versions of all three photocopiable pages.
● Answers to all three photocopiable pages.
● Interactive version of 'Adding s, es and ves'.

Name:

**Plurals and compound words**

# Adding s, es and ves

■ Do these word sums to make plural answers. Remember to use the plural spelling rules.

■ Make up and illustrate your own word sums in the blank spaces.

one + one = two _____

one + one = two _____

one + one = two _____

one + one = two _____

one + one = two _____

one + one = two _____

one + one = two _____

one + one = two _____

one + one = two _____

one [ ] + one [ ] = two _____

one [ ] + one [ ] = two _____

■ Write the rules you came across on a piece of paper or in your notebook.

**PHOTOCOPIABLE**  ■SCHOLASTIC www.scholastic.co.uk

**Plurals and compound words**

# Plural rules

■ Complete this crossword by making plurals from the words in the word bank at the bottom of the page. All the answers are plural nouns.

**Tip:** Remember the plural rules and watch out for exceptions.

**Across**

5. Steep rocks by the sea (6)
7. Tricks or deceptions (6)
9. Kings or queens (8)
10. Large water birds with webbed feet (5)
12. Thick-leaved desert plants that store water (5)
13. People who steal things (7)
14. Animals with long ears that look like a small horse (7)

**Down**

1. Buses used on long journeys (7)
2. Small, furry animals with a long tail (4)
3. Keyboard instruments with black and white keys (6)
4. Fairies often grant three of these (6)
6. Criminals often tried to hide theirs (who they are) (10)
8. Sounds that repeat because they are reflected (6)
11. These animals give us wool (5)

| identity | goose | hoax | piano | mouse |
| thief | monarch | cactus | echo | cliff |
| sheep | donkey | wish | coach | |

**SCHOLASTIC**
www.scholastic.co.uk      **PHOTOCOPIABLE**                               **Scholastic English Skills**
Spelling and vocabulary: Year 5    **65**

Name:

# Compound word battleships

- Use your set of root words to make five compound words of your choice.
- Write your words into the grid, either vertically or horizontally.
- Use your words to play battleships with a partner.

**Tip:** Remember to hide your grid from your partner.

| | 1 | 2 | 3 | 4 | 5 | 6 | 7 | 8 | 9 | 10 | 11 | 12 |
|---|---|---|---|---|---|---|---|---|---|---|---|---|
| m | | | | | | | | | | | | |
| l | | | | | | | | | | | | |
| k | | | | | | | | | | | | |
| j | | | | | | | | | | | | |
| i | | | | | | | | | | | | |
| h | | | | | | | | | | | | |
| g | | | | | | | | | | | | |
| f | | | | | | | | | | | | |
| e | | | | | | | | | | | | |
| d | | | | | | | | | | | | |
| c | | | | | | | | | | | | |
| b | | | | | | | | | | | | |
| a | | | | | | | | | | | | |

## Root words – set 1

| | |
|---|---|
| proof | honey |
| comb | light |
| brief | hood |
| child | ground |
| moon | chop |
| back | sound |
| stick | case |

## Root words – set 2

| | |
|---|---|
| knife | work |
| house | pen |
| dress | fall |
| break | day |
| night | head |
| home | play |
| ache | fast |

# Word families

To understand how words are related in form and meaning.

## Background knowledge

The words in a word family are normally related to each other by a combination of morphology, grammar and meaning. Whether related by morphology, grammar, meaning or a combination, a word family always has an 'anchor' word, which when related by morphology or grammar tends to be known as a root word; when the words are linked by meaning alone, the links tend to be through synonyms or similar, with a focus on a thesaurus rather than a dictionary. Word families related by morphology and/or grammar are especially useful for helping children spell more accurately, in addition to which, knowledge of the spellings and meanings of root words, prefixes and suffixes helps children not only spell but also understand extended words within a word family. For example, knowing the root word *mobile* (meaning movable) will help children to spell other words in the same family: *mobility, mobilise, mobilisation, immobile, immobility*.

## Activities

● **Photocopiable page 68 'Find my family'**
Discuss inflectional suffixes and how root words with inflectional suffixes make a form of word family. Ask the role of each suffix. Show that more than one suffix can be added and that spelling rules apply. Find out what the children understand by the suffix 'ish'. Explain that *it indicates approximation*. The suffix can also mean *having the quality of* as in babyish. What do the children notice about adjectives that end in 'e' when 'ish' is added? Ask the children to use some examples in sentences.

● **Photocopiable page 69 'Related words'**
To fill in the crossword grid, the children use clues based on root words. Support less confident children by filling in one or two of the words before copying the page.

Challenge more confident spellers by filling in the word *alphabetical* (answer to 1 down) as a starting point, but mask the numbers before they begin.

● **Photocopiable page 70 'The Sign family'**
*Sign* is the root of many words. It can take both inflectional and derivational suffixes as well as prefixes that alter its meaning. The children must identify the words containing *sign* somewhere in the word and write them in the cloud. Draw their attention to the spelling tip using a couple of the words, such as *sign* and *signal*. The non-silent 'g' is very helpful for spelling. Invite children to identify words they are unfamiliar with, to look them up and then to write out the word with its definition.

## Further ideas

● **Personal collections:** As the children engage in personal reading, ask them to add the words they meet that are derived from root words to their personal word banks.
● **Family gatherings:** Choose a word family of the week. Put up a chart (such as a chain of people from a repeatedly folded outline) with the family root in the first section. Get the class to come up with a list of related words, identifying what has been added. Build the family during the week. You can choose inflectional, derivational or spelling-pattern families.
● **Find someone like me:** Choose a word of the week and invite children to find words with a similar meaning (synonyms) to extend vocabulary. This can be done with or without a thesaurus to make it more or less challenging.

## Digital content

On the digital component you will find:
● Printable versions of all three photocopiable pages.
● Answers to all three photocopiable pages.

Name:

# Word families

# Find my family

■ Help *develop* and *occupy* find their family members by choosing suffixes from the box to add to them.

■ Write your new words around each root word and then underline the suffix you added. Watch out for spelling rules.

| er | ment | s | ing | ed | able | al | ation |

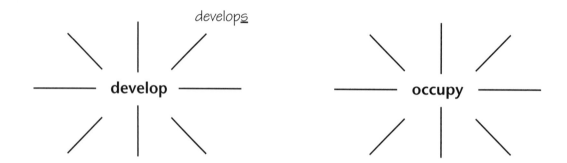

Some word families are created when you add the same suffix to different root words – they become related by suffix.

Adjective + **ish** = adjective, *an approximation*

Noun + **ish** = adjective, *having the quality of*

■ Make these words by adding **ish** to an adjective.

Someone quite tall = _____

Something quite blue = _____

Something quite big = _____

Something almost sweet = _____

■ Add **ish** to these nouns to create adjectives.

fool + ish = _____     tickle + ish = _____

child + ish = _____     style + ish = _____

baby + ish = _____     red + ish = _____

## Word families

# Related words

- Use the clues to write the related word in the crossword.
- Use a dictionary to check the spellings.

**Across**
2. Adjective related to the noun *fact*.
4. Adjective related to the noun *energy*.
6. Adjective related to the noun *system*.
7. Adjective related to the noun *strength*.
8. Adverb related to the adjective *individual*.

**Down**
1. Adjective to describe the order of the *alphabet*.
3. Noun root of *persuade*.
4. Noun linked to the verb *explain*.
5. Adjective formed from the noun *rhyme*.

Name:

## Word families

# The Sign family

■  Read the words in the box aloud.

■  Write any words that belong to the same word family as *sign* in the cloud below and then underline the root word.

| | | | |
|---|---|---|---|
| sacrifice | resign | sincere | signed |
| signature | signs | insignificant | style |
| insignia | aspire | spine | desperate |
| decide | signing | recognise | assign |
| design | destroy | designate | significant |
| correspond | assignation | reside | system |
| unsigned | designation | signify | signal |

**Tip:** Which letter is silent in *sign*? What happens when you say *signature*?

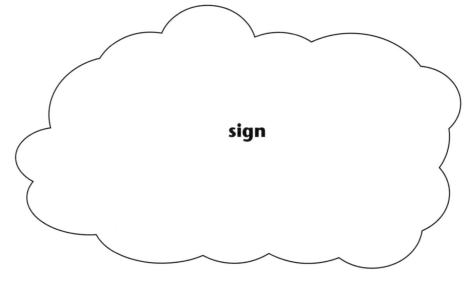

sign

■  Use a dictionary to look up any words in the family that are unfamiliar to you. Write the words followed by their definitions below. Then discuss with a partner how they relate to *sign*.

_____      _____

_____      _____

_____      _____

_____      _____

# Greek and Latin roots

## Objective

To investigate the use and spelling of prefixes and suffixes with Greek and Latin origins.

## Background knowledge

English spelling borrows from other languages including Latin and Greek. An understanding of the meaning of Greek and Latin prefixes will help children to spell many words in English. Understanding the history of a word is as important as morphology in enabling successful spelling. Etymological knowledge is like a code for spelling; for example, knowing that the grapheme 'ph' came from the Greek language means knowing that Greek origin words with the phoneme /f/ are spelled 'ph' not 'f' or 'ff'. Furthermore, prefixes added to a root word predictably alter its meaning: 'anti' (against: derived originally from Greek) + 'septic' (containing or resulting from disease-causing organisms: derived from Greek via Latin) = 'antiseptic'. Knowledge of these word 'building blocks' helps children decode challenging words such as *antipathy*.

## Activities

● **Photocopiable page 72 'Latin prefixes'**
Discuss the meaning of the Latin prefixes. Create a spider diagram of words the children know containing each prefix to establish and consolidate the meaning of each and to help children with a restricted vocabulary. Demonstrate that adding a prefix rarely changes the spelling of the root word. Let the children use dictionaries to match the prefixes and root words to create complete words and find their definitions.
● **Photocopiable page 73 'Greek roots'**
As a class, study the Greek prefix table. Discuss familiar words and record them on the board. Let the children use a dictionary to help match the prefixes to their definitions. Note that most of these words do not have a recognisable English root, so demonstrate how knowing

the prefix can be a strategy not only for decoding the meaning of unfamiliar or complex words but also for spelling them. Children should then find other words containing the selection of prefixes and write out their definitions on a piece of paper to test the rest of the class during the plenary session.
● **Photocopiable page 74 'Number prefixes'**
This activity introduces commonly used prefixes denoting number when affixed to other nouns, adjectives and adverbs. Link to the children's existing knowledge by using familiar words such as those commonly used in mathematics, for example, *triangle*. Remind the children they will find it easier to work out the word definitions and spell correctly if they can identify and remember the meaning of a wide range of prefixes and roots.

## Further ideas

● **Set in stone:** Make a display of a Roman amphitheatre or a Greek temple. Let the children decorate them with stones containing Latin or Greek derived words. Encourage them to colour words sharing the same root or prefix similarly.
● **Shared and independent reading:** Encourage the children to note words with Greek and Latin origins as they read, so as to recognise recurring roots and prefixes to use as an inbuilt strategy for improving both their spelling and their vocabulary. This bonding of etymology, meaning and spelling is especially valuable to children with less well-developed visual recall of word spelling.
● **Other curriculum areas:** Encourage the children to collect words with Greek and Latin origins from work in other curriculum areas (for example, Mathematics, Geography and Science). Demonstrate through their collections how critical etymology is for both understanding and spelling words correctly. Choose a curriculum area each week as a focus.

## Digital content

On the digital component you will find:
● Printable versions of all three photocopiable pages.
● Answers to all three photocopiable pages.
● Interactive version of 'Greek roots'.

Greek and Latin roots

# Latin prefixes

■ Read the list of prefixes and their meanings. Now look at the root words and choose a prefix to match each one. Write a definition of the word you have created (use a dictionary if you are unsure).

■ Use a dictionary (or your own knowledge) to add another interesting word with the same prefix to your list.

**Tip:** Notice whether adding the prefix changes the spelling of the root word.

| Latin prefix | Root word | New word | Definition | Extra word |
|---|---|---|---|---|
| aque (water) | navigate | | | |
| un (not) | port | | | |
| trans (across) | sonic | | | |
| dis (apart) | duct | | | |
| bene (good/well) | script | | | |
| post (after) | sect | | | |
| sub (under) | lateral | | | |
| super (above) | necessary | | | |
| bi (two) | merge | | | |
| circum (around) | factor | | | |

**Greek and Latin roots**

# Greek roots

■ Read the list of Greek prefixes and root words, their basic meanings and an example of a word containing each one. Then match the prefixes and roots to their definitions below.

■ Use a dictionary to find another word containing each prefix or root and write a sentence using it on a separate piece of paper. Underline the prefix or root.

| Greek prefix/root | Basic meaning | Example word |
|---|---|---|
| anthrop | human | anthropology |
| chron | time | chronicle |
| dem/demo | people | democracy |
| dia | across/apart/through | dialogue |
| mono | one/single/alone | monotone |
| morph | form | morphology |
| path | feeling/disease | pathology |
| philo/phil | loving/attracted to | philharmonic |
| peri | around | perimeter |
| para | beside/near | parasite |

1. Study of human beings and their evolution: _____

2. Sound that is continuous or repeated on one note: _____

3. Record of events in time order of happening: _____

4. Study of the form or makeup of words: _____

5. Outer edge or border of an area or shape: _____

6. Devoted to or appreciative of music: _____

7. Scientific study of diseases and causes of death: _____

8. Organism living on and off another living being: _____

9. Conversation between two people: _____

10. A government of people elected by the people: _____

Name:

## Greek and Latin roots

# Number prefixes

We use Greek and Latin prefixes in adjectives, adverbs and nouns relating to numbers. For example, the Latin prefix **bi** means *two* as in *bicycle,* a cycle with **two** wheels.

■ Understanding a prefix's meaning helps you spell the word. Read the prefixes below and see how many you recognise from words you already know.

**Tip:** You might recognise some from maths.

| Prefix | Basic meaning | Origin |
|--------|---------------|--------|
| uni | one | Latin |
| mono | one | Greek |
| bi | two | Latin |
| di | two | Greek |
| du | two | Latin |
| hemi | half | Greek |
| semi | half | Latin |
| tri | three | Latin and Greek |
| quad | four | Latin |
| quart | four | Latin |
| quin | five | Latin |
| penta | five | Greek |
| hex | six | Greek |
| sex | six | Latin |
| hept | seven | Greek |
| oct | eight | Latin and Greek |
| non | nine | Latin |
| dec | ten | Latin and Greek |
| cent | hundred | Latin |
| mill | thousand | Latin |

■ On a separate piece of paper, write each word below with its definition next to it. Check your answers in a dictionary.

| | | | |
|---|---|---|---|
| decathlon | monologue | duplicate | semicircle |
| hemisphere | biennial | unique | dilemma |
| quarterly | triplicate | quintet | nonagenarian |
| millennium | quadruped | sextuplets | century |
| pentangle | hexagon | octopus | heptathlete |

# Dig back to the roots

To build words from prefixes, roots and suffixes and to identify roots within words to support spelling.

## Background knowledge

A morpheme is the smallest linguistic unit that has meaning. For example, 'unhelpful' comprises the morphemes 'un', 'help' and 'ful': 'un' and 'ful' are *bound morphemes* – they are not words in their own right; 'help' is a *free morpheme* because it is a word in its own right. Roots, such as 'path' (feeling, disease) are derived from other languages. Although not actual words, they do form word roots (and so count as morphemes). Emphasise that the root can be the beginning, at the end or in the middle of a word. Knowing root meanings is advantageous for children for decoding complex words and learning their spellings. The root is the most important part of a word in terms of meaning. As many English words are borrowed or derived from other languages, focusing on roots allows children to see how words are made up and use this knowledge to understand and spell new words.

## Activities

● **Photocopiable page 76 'Building from the root up'**
Invite the children to work with a partner and a dictionary to collect words that contain the roots on the photocopiable sheet. Share the first example and discuss the words given. Can they disassemble them and identify the root, as well as the prefixes and suffixes? Demonstrate how knowing that 'ph' makes the /f/ sound in many words with Greek roots can assist with spelling as does recognising the entire root (*graph*), inside a more complex word. Remind them that suffix spelling rules still apply. Note that the 'b' in *scribe* can become 'p' (*script*).

● **Photocopiable page 77 'Root work'**
Display a set of words with a foreign root (Greek or Latin) on the board, such as *reject, inject, interject,*

*project, dejected*. Discuss the meaning of each word, using an online dictionary on the whiteboard if possible. Establish a meaning for the root by deciding what each definition has in common ('ject', meaning *throw* or *cast*). Explain that these roots are derivations and don't necessarily form stand-alone words. Let the children work with a partner to do the same activity for the word groups on the photocopiable sheet.

● **Photocopiable page 78 'Root for France'**
Read the words in the central box. Can the children find any part of the word that looks or sounds like the French words in the surrounding boxes? Sort the words into the correct boxes.

## Further ideas

● **What do I mean?:** Give the children a list of foreign roots, such as: *octo, form, sphere* or *mania* and ask them to find as many words as they can which use them. Can they work out what the root means from the words?

● **Tree of knowledge:** Draw a large tree with roots underground. On the roots, write lots of root words, particularly those of Latin and Greek origin. Display the tree on an accessible wall and place beside it a box of paper leaves, a dictionary and writing materials. Encourage the children to find words which can be built using the root words. Let them write the word on a leaf with their name and add it to the tree.

● **Root race:** Put up a root word such as *colour* and challenge the children to come up with as many words as possible in pairs using the root.

## Digital content

On the digital component you will find:
● Printable versions of all three photocopiable pages.
● Answers to all three photocopiable pages.
● Interactive version of 'Root for France'.

Name:

# Building from the root up

■ Work with a partner to discuss and look up words that contain the roots listed below. The first one has been started for you.

1. graph (from the Greek **graphein**, *write or record*)

graphic, autograph, graphite, geography, paragraph…

2. act (from the Latin **actus**, *a doing, act or performance*)

_____

3. audit (from the Latin **auditus**, *an act of hearing*)

_____

4. tact (from the Latin **tactus**, *a sense of touch*)

_____

5. potent (from the Latin **potens**, *powerful*)

_____

6. form (from the Latin **forma**, *shape*)

_____

7. scribe (from the Latin **scribere**, *to write*)

_____

8. photo (from the Greek **phos**, *light*)

_____

9. auto (from the Greek **autos**, *self*)

_____

10. acid (from the Latin **acidus**, *sour, vinegar*)

_____

**Dig back to the roots**

# Root work

■ These words have Latin or Greek roots but the root is not a word that we use on its own. Read each set of three words containing the same root. Write a definition for each word. Underline the common root, write it in the box and then find out its meaning.

■ Can you find another word for each root you have investigated?

| Word | Meaning | Root and its meaning |
|---|---|---|
| interrupt | | |
| rupture | | |
| corrupt | | |
| ignite | | |
| ignition | | |
| igneous | | |
| inspect | | |
| spectator | | |
| aspect | | |
| injunction | | |
| conjunction | | |
| juncture | | |
| punctuation | | |
| acupuncture | | |
| puncture | | |

Name:

**Dig back to the roots**

# Root for France

Many words with French origins or roots end in **et**. We pronounce this ending in two ways: *ballet* – like **ay** in *play*; *blanket* – like **it** in *pit*.

| | | | | | | |
|---|---|---|---|---|---|---|
| trumpet | sorbet | bouquet | crumpet | fillet | bracket | ticket |
| | cabaret | buffet | cornet | ferret | sachet | |
| | | millet | gourmet | banquet | | |

■ Say each word aloud, then write it on the correct memory note.

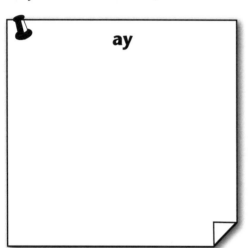

**ay**

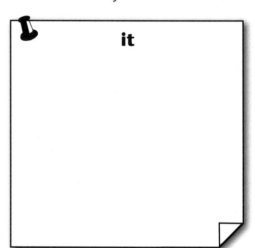

**it**

■ The **ch** spelling is pronounced in different ways. Say each word aloud and sort the words into the right column according to their original roots (and sounds).

| | | | | |
|---|---|---|---|---|
| orchid | chaperone | echo | orchestra | brochure |
| chaos | cliché | chorus | charade | anchor | cachet |
| monarchy | chandelier | stomach | architect | quiche |
| parachute | chivalry | chic | technology | |

| **ch** pronounced **k** (Greek) | **ch** pronounced **sh** (French) |
|---|---|
| *ache* | *chef* |
| | |

# Assessment

## Assessment grid

The following grid shows the main objectives and activities covered in this chapter. You can use the grid to locate activities that cover a particular focus that you are keen to monitor.

| Objective | Page | Activity title |
|---|---|---|
| To use knowledge of morphology and etymology in spelling. | 60 | Back to roots |
| | 61 | Word maths |
| | 62 | Root it out |
| | 64 | Adding s, es and ves |
| | 65 | Plural rules |
| | 66 | Compound word battleships |
| | 68 | Find my family |
| | 69 | Related words |
| | 70 | The Sign family |
| | 72 | Latin prefixes |
| | 73 | Greek roots |
| | 74 | Number prefixes |
| | 76 | Building from the root up |
| | 77 | Root work |
| | 78 | Root for France |
| To revise word family work to aid spelling. | 68 | Find my family |
| | 69 | Related words |
| | 70 | The Sign family |
| To use further prefixes and suffixes and understand the guidelines for using them. | 72 | Latin prefixes |
| | 73 | Greek roots |
| | 74 | Number prefixes |

## Observation and record keeping

Watch out for children who alter the spelling of root words when adding prefixes, particularly where the added prefix creates a double letter. Learning the meaning and spelling patterns of Greek and Latin prefixes and suffixes will help children to avoid common spelling mistakes. While the children are completing the photocopiable sheets in this chapter, encourage them to keep a spelling journal. Encourage them to write down words that were tricky for them and any mistakes

they made. A note of appropriate rules, patterns and mnemonics will also be helpful to them, together with a reminder of the word's origins and any related words or words with a similar grapheme–phoneme correspondence. Use the spelling journals to provide evidence for assessing ongoing work. Note that visual and kinaesthetic memory are more important to some children than others, so praise any alternative strategies and record them to share with the class.

## Assessment activity

● **What you need**
Photocopiable page 80 'Word building' for each child, A4 paper, writing materials.
● **What to do**
Ask the children to work independently to answer each of the three sections. Before they begin, check that they have understood what is required of them in each section.

## Differentiation

● Go through each section of the assessment activity orally with less confident learners before they attempt them independently.
● Challenge more confident learners by asking them to add an extra word in the first section and to add more words to the trees in section two – even by adding prefixes as well. Challenge them further by limiting the time allowed to complete the assessment sheet.

## Further learning

● **Greek or Latin:** Encourage the children to think carefully about words with Greek or Latin prefixes and suffixes when reading and writing in other areas of the curriculum.
● **Writing:** Provide the children with a list of six of the words from the photocopiable sheets and challenge them to write them into a paragraph or a sentence.

Name:

## Assessment

# Word building

■ Write a word that begins with each of these Greek or Latin prefixes.

auto _____     kilo _____

micro _____    aqua _____

bene _____     multi _____

mill _____     dia _____

■ Complete these word families by adding suffixes to each root.

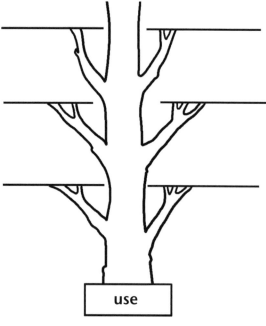

use

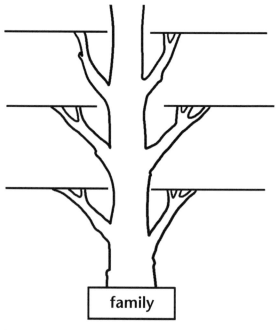

family

■ Find the following words all containing the French root 'mort'.

A **noun** and its opposite _____ _____

An **adjective** and its opposite _____ _____

An **adverb** _____

**Verb** meaning to cause to feel shame or hurt the pride of _____

**Synonym** for an undertaker (person who organises funerals) _____

**Verb** meaning to make someone live forever (make famous) _____

A **noun** – number of deaths in particular period or place _____

**I think the French root *mort* means** _____.

# Chapter 5

# Homophones and other tricky words

## Introduction

The word *homophone* is derived from Greek and means 'the same sound'. Two or more different words are homophones if they sound exactly the same when pronounced. They are often confusing and cause spelling errors. The trick is to remember which spelling goes with which meaning. Sometimes there is a slight difference in the sound of the word like *advise* and *advice*. These words are called near homophones and can be difficult to spot because they rely on correct pronunciation. When dealing with silent letters, note that some letters that are no longer sounded used to be sounded hundreds of years ago, like the word *knight*. The 'gh' used to represent the sound that 'ch' now represents in the Scottish word *loch*. For further practice, please see the 'Homophones and other tricky words' section in the Year 5 workbook.

## In this chapter

## Poster notes

**Don't be fooled (page 82)**
Emphasise that the children need to be on the lookout for tricky words because they are out bound to catch them out. Use the poster as a visual aid in your lessons. Encourage the children to add to the poster, especially with words that have caught them out. They can cut out each section of the poster and stick them onto separate pages in their books providing more space for their own words.

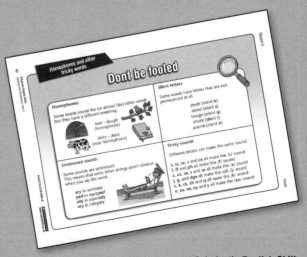

# Dont be fooled

## Homophones

Some words sound like (or almost like) other words but they have a different meaning.

*bow – bough*
(homophone)

*dairy – diary*
(near homophone)

## Silent letters

Some words have letters that are not pronounced at all.

*doubt* (silent **b**)
*island* (silent **s**)
*foreign* (silent **g**)
*thistle* (silent **t**)
*solemn* (silent **n**)

## Unstressed sounds

Some sounds are unstressed. This means that some letter strings aren't obvious when you say the word.

**ary** in *secretary*
**ped** in *equipped*
**ally** in *especially*
**ory** in *category*

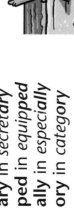

## Tricky sounds

Different letters can make the same sound:

**s, ss, se, c** and **ce** all make the **/s/** sound
**f, ff** and **ph** all make the **/f/** sound
**z, zz, ze, s** and **se** all make the **/z/** sound
**j, g,** and **dge** all make the soft **/j/** sound
**c, k, ck, ch** and **q** all make the **/k/** sound
**e, ea, ee, ey** and **y** all make the **/ee/** sound

# Homophones

## Objective

To spell homophones.

## Background knowledge

There are many words in English that have very similar sounds but different spellings and can be easily confused. It can help children differentiate between confusing pairs of words when they investigate their meaning and use and work out their own memory tricks for using them accurately. Looking for words within words can help, as can identifying the tricky parts of one of the words and making up a rhyme, acrostic or other mnemonic about the tricky bit. Looking at word families is also useful. The word *alter* becomes *alteration* and is linked to *alternate*. This helps to distinguish it from the word *altar*. Children should also be aware of the word class of a word as sometimes the spelling helps us to know the word class. Words that end with 'ce' are usually nouns (as in *practice*) while words ending 'se' are usually verbs (as in *practise*).

## Activities

● **Photocopiable page 84 'Which one won?'**
The children choose between pairs of sentences to decide which one uses a homophone correctly. They write the words in their spelling journal with their own definitions to help them to differentiate between the words. Before beginning the activity, ask the children to brainstorm some homophones that they already know. Point out that the sound of the word out of context gives no clues to its meaning and so no clues to its spelling, therefore context is important.
● **Photocopiable page 85 'Right it write'**
Begin by asking the children if they have ever noticed a spelling error in a newspaper, an advert or a poster. Sometimes a spelling error is used for effect, but mostly it is careless. Remind the children that correct spelling is important, particularly if the purpose is formal and public. Let them find the errors in the notices, cross them out and write the correct word.

● **Photocopiable page 86 'Homophone riddle'**
Words that sound the same have no meaning without a context and there is no way to distinguish the spelling. The children can use the clues (or riddles) to work out words that sound the same. Begin by giving the class a few verbal examples such as *something done on paper* and *the opposite of wrong*. As a fun revision activity, let them work in pairs taking turns to ask each other a homophone riddle. Answers should be written to give them more spelling practice.

## Further ideas

● **Circle time:** With a small group of children, draw up a list of four simple homophones (for example, *to*, *too* and *two*). Ask one child to use the first word in a sentence – for example, *I am going to school*. The next child should extend the sentence by adding *too* (*I am going to school and my sister is going too*) and the third child then adds a phrase that includes *two* (*I am going to school and my sister is going too so I hope there is space in your car for two of us*).
● **Bingo:** The children should make a Bingo board, filling their board with ten homophones. Once they have prepared their boards, give them a word in context and if they have the word, they should cross it out. The first child to cross out a row calls 'Bingo'. Let the game continue until someone has crossed off all their words.

## Digital content

On the digital component you will find:
● Printable versions of all three photocopiable pages.
● Answers to all three photocopiable pages.
● Interactive versions of 'Which one won?' and 'Write it right'.

Name:

## Homophones

# Which one won?

■ Read these pairs of sentences. Put a tick next to the correct use of the word and then check your answer with a dictionary.

1. Take care you don't **brake** the glass. ☐
   Take care you don't **break** the glass. ☐

2. The cross-country **course** was very challenging. ☐
   The cross-country **coarse** was very challenging. ☐

3. Danny ate the **whole** meal far too quickly and felt ill. ☐
   Danny ate the **hole** meal far too quickly and felt ill. ☐

4. She wrote a **draught** for her story before typing it up on a computer. ☐
   She wrote a **draft** for her story before typing it up on a computer. ☐

5. Make sure you eat all your **serial** for breakfast. ☐
   Make sure you eat all your **cereal** for breakfast. ☐

6. The school **principal** made a speech to all the parents. ☐
   The school **principle** made a speech to all the parents. ☐

7. The building was reinforced with **steal**. ☐
   The building was reinforced with **steel**. ☐

8. Don't forget to pack your **stationary** for school. ☐
   Don't forget to pack your **stationery** for school. ☐

9. That was a lovely **compliment**. Thank you. ☐
   That was a lovely **complement**. Thank you. ☐

10. I don't think you **heard** what I said. ☐
    I don't think you **herd** what I said. ☐

■ Copy each of the confusable words into your spelling journal and write your own definition for each one.

## Homophones

# Write it right

Homophones can catch us out and cause silly mistakes in obvious places.

■  Find the errors in these notices. Cross out the incorrect words and write them correctly on the lines below.

**Tip: ce/cy** endings are used for nouns while **se/sy** endings are used for verbs.

| NOTICE | NOTICE | NOTICE |
|---|---|---|
| Please bough when the king enters. | Soccer practise is cancelled. | Queue here to renew your license. |

_____
_____
_____

| NOTICE | NOTICE | NOTICE |
|---|---|---|
| Principle's office – no entry. | Silent area. Please keep the piece. | Assembly will be held tomorrow mourning. |

_____
_____
_____

| NOTICE | NOTICE | NOTICE |
|---|---|---|
| No fighting aloud. | Please take care when you pore the paint. | Do not pick the flours. |

_____
_____
_____

Name:

## Homophones

# Homophone riddle

■ Use the clues below to work out the words. Remember that both words should sound the same. Check your answers in a dictionary.

1. a. Extra distance                              _____

    b. A male parent                              _____

2. a. A visitor                                   _____

    b. You didn't know the answer, so you…     _____

3. a. Before noon                                 _____

    b. Grieving                                 _____

4. a. A herb                                      _____

    b. Ticking away                             _____

5. a. A type of table in a church                 _____

    b. To change                                _____

6. a. A heavy metal                               _____

    b. Past tense of to be in front             _____

7. a. A first attempt at writing something        _____

    b. A current of air                         _____

8. a. A moral truth or belief                     _____

    b. The lead performer                       _____

9. a. A mark on the skin                          _____

    b. A process when making tea               _____

10. a. Out loud                                   _____

     b. Permitted                               _____

# Easily confused

To spell words that are easily confused.

## Background knowledge

Words that sound almost the same but are not quite the same sound are called near homophones. The difference is slight but the meaning and function of the word is completely different. These words with a similar sound may be easily confused, especially if incorrectly pronounced (like the words *peas* and *peace*). For this reason it is important to check that the children use the correct pronunciation. Using the word in context will help to reinforce the difference in sound and meaning. Continue to use mnemonics like word associations, rhymes or pictures that may help them associate the spelling with their meanings. Words with an apostrophe are sometimes confused with other words, those with ''ve': *should've* and *could've* sound like 'should of' or 'could of' but are really 'should have' and 'could have'. The other tricky pair, *it's* and *its*, can be confusing because the apostrophe indicates a contraction and not possession.

## Activities

● **Photocopiable page 88 'Near homophones'**
Ask the children for examples of words that sound almost the same. Discuss the importance of correct pronunciation. Go through the words on the photocopiable sheet, making sure that they are pronounced correctly. The children use dictionaries to check the meaning of the words before deciding which word is correct in the context. Once this is done, encourage them to find a letter clue in each sentence to help remember the correct word. For example, in the first sentence, the 'e' in *medicine* reminds us to use /e/ for *effect*. Get them to explain the association to a partner.

● **Photocopiable page 89 'Apostrophe confusion'**
Use this as an opportunity to revise the apostrophe of omission. If children understand the purpose of the apostrophe, they should be less inclined to confuse the words. Highlight the pronunciation of apostrophe 've' in words like *should've*, *would've*, *could've* as these are sometimes incorrectly pronounced 'should of' etc. 'It's' is a contraction, while 'its' indicates possession.

● **Photocopiable page 90 'What's my definition?'**
In this activity, the children use a dictionary to find the definitions of pairs of easily confused words and write a sentence for each word to demonstrate the correct usage. An understanding of each word's meaning and word family will help children differentiate between easily confused words. After they have finished the activity, ask them to compare the sentences they wrote.

## Further ideas

● **Confusable cards:** Create word cards using easily confused words. Place them face down. Invite a small group of children to take turns to pick a card. If they can use the word correctly in a sentence, the card can be removed. If used incorrectly, it is replaced face down.
● **Leave a clue:** The children make up sentences with hidden clues to help them remember confusing words. Once they have made ten sentences, let them swap and have a go at working out someone else's clues.
● **Words at work:** Turn word pairs into pictures or diagrams showing the words in action. The word *device* can be put into a vice, while *advise* could be in a thought bubble. Turn them into classroom posters and display them. You can use this idea to complete the activity on page 90 instead of writing sentences.

## Digital content

On the digital component you will find:
● Printable versions of all three photocopiable pages.
● Answers to 'Near homophones' and 'Apostrophe confusion'.
● Interactive versions of 'Near homophones' and 'Apostrophe confusion'.

Name:

## Easily confused

# Near homophones

- Read these pairs of words aloud. They sound similar but not exactly the same.
- Check their definitions then fill in the correct word in each sentence.

**affect or effect**
The medicine he gave me had little _____. I still feel ill.

**advice or advise**
I don't know what to revise. Please can you _____ me.

**device or devise**
To fix the computer I need a certain _____.

**farther or further**
Tennis club is cancelled until _____ notice.

**precede or proceed**
In an emergency follow the arrows and _____ to the exit.

**wary or weary**
The athlete felt _____ after completing the race.

**eligible or illegible**
Her excellent essay is _____ for the prize.

**dairy or diary**
Did you know that the Tooth Fairy lives on a _____ farm?

**breath or breathe**
Before you begin to seethe, _____ deeply and try to relax.

**insure or ensure**
Before you travel please _____ your important belongings.

- Now go back and circle the hidden letter clue in each sentence

**PHOTOCOPIABLE**

SCHOLASTIC
www.scholastic.co.uk

## Easily confused

# Apostrophe confusion

■ Write out the contractions below in full. Find the word in the word bank that each contraction is easily confused with and write it in the final column.

**Tip:** Sometimes, words with an apostrophe sound like other words.

| there | its | your | whose | weave |
|-------|-----|------|-------|-------|
| his | were | wheel | aisle | |

| Contraction | Words in full | Easily confused with: |
|-------------|---------------|------------------------|
| it's | | |
| they're | | |
| you're | | |
| who's | | |
| we're | | |
| I'll | | |
| we'll | | |
| he's | | |
| we've | | |

■ Delete the incorrect word options in each sentence.

1. Don't forget to label **you're/your** luggage or **they're/there** going to wonder **whose/who's** it is.

2. **You're/Your** going to enjoy **you're/your** holiday. **It's/Its** a lovely place.

3. With all that rain over **there/they're**, **we're/were** going to need umbrellas.

Name:

## Easily confused

# What's my definition?

■  Look up these words in a dictionary. Find their word family and write the definition.

■  Use the back of this page to write a sentence for each of these words to show their meaning.

| Easily confused words | Word family | Dictionary definition |
|---|---|---|
| accept | | |
| except | | |
| angel | | |
| angle | | |
| allusion | | |
| illusion | | |
| desert | | |
| dessert | | |
| loose | | |
| lose | | |
| ascent | | |
| accent | | |
| guessed | | |
| guest | | |
| descent | | |
| dissent | | |

# Silent letters

### Objective

To spell some words with silent letters.

### Background knowledge

Apart from word games and visual clues, rules can help make silent letters memorable.
- **Silent 'k':** Silent 'k' is always at the beginning of a word and always has an 'n' after it.
- **Silent 'g':** 'g' is silent when it partners with 'n' ('gn') at the beginning or end of a word.
- **Silent 'h':** 'h' is silent when partnered with 'w', 'r', 'c', 'g' and 'x'. It is also silent at the end of a word when it follows a vowel and in words where it is between two vowels.
- **Silent 'b':** 'b' is usually silent when partnered with 'm' or 't' at the end of a word.
- **Silent 'l':** Silent 'l' goes after the phonemes /a/, /oa/ and /oo/.
- **Silent 's':** Silent 's' always follows the vowel 'i'.
- **Silent 'c':** 'c' is silent when it partners with 's'.
- **Silent 'gh':** 'gh' has no sound of its own. It is silent when followed by 't' and when a word ends with 'ough'.
- **Silent 'n':** 'n' is silent in the combination 'mn' at the end of a word.
- **Silent 't':** Silent 't' always follows 's'.

### Activities

- **Photocopiable page 92 'Picture it'**
Let the children have fun thinking of words with silent letters that match the pictures. Then, encourage them to say each word aloud so they can hear which letter isn't said. Draw their attention to where the silent letter falls in the word. Is there any pattern? Make up rhymes with the silent letter words or simply say lots of words with the same silent letter 'saying it silly'.

- **Photocopiable page 93 'Silent letter sort'**
Ask the children to work with a partner to copy all the words onto blank cards as well as writing the letters 'k', 'h', 'c', 'g', 's', 'n', 't' and 'b' onto individual cards (you need 48 cards). Ask them to double-check the spellings before they play, using the opportunity to reinforce which are the silent letters. The first game provides an opportunity to clear up any misconceptions about pronunciation or meaning. In the second game it is important that the children say the word they are laying down and that they identify the silent letter.

- **Photocopiable page 94 'Can you see it?'**
Let the children work out which silent letters are missing in the words and fill them in. Encourage them to group the words into pairs with the same silent letters. Check if they can recall any rules or tips for using silent letters.

### Further ideas

- **Make it memorable:** Silent letters are tricky and need to be highlighted in order for them to become memorable. It is important that children have oral practice in 'saying it silly' in order to hear the silent letter. Singing 'Getting to k-know you' and other songs is one such approach.
- **Make the rules:** Refer to 'Silent letter sort' photocopiable page. Once they have sorted the words and identified the common silent letter, let them come up with their own rules for using each silent letter.
- **Snap:** Use the word cards from 'Silent letter sort' to play the game 'snap' in pairs. Letter cards should be included. Players divide the cards between them. At the same time, both players play a card facing up. The first player to call 'snap' when both cards have the same silent letter, wins the cards. The winner is the player with the most cards.

### Digital content

On the digital component you will find:
- Printable versions of all three photocopiable pages.
- Answers to 'Silent letter sort' and 'Can you see it?'.
- Interactive version of 'Silent letter sort'.

Name:

**Silent letters**

# Picture it

■ Label each picture using the silent letter.

| d | g | l | p |
|---|---|---|---|
| Monday Tuesday ? Thursday | | | |
| _____ | _____ | _____ | _____ |

| k | h | ch | gh |
|---|---|---|---|
| | | | |
| _____ | _____ | _____ | _____ |

| s | n | t | b |
|---|---|---|---|
| | | | |
| _____ | _____ | _____ | _____ |

■ Think of a funny way of remembering the silent letters. It helps to 'say it silly' by saying the missing letter so you can fix it in your mind. Have a go!

## Silent letters

# Silent letter sort

| | | | | |
|---|---|---|---|---|
| knight | crumb | subtle | listen | environment |
| lamb | doubt | muscle | rhythm | column |
| whistle | castle | thistle | island | neighbour |
| knit | hymn | vehicle | ancient | conscious |
| fasten | loch | rhyme | foreign | knowledge |
| government | lightning | stomach | yacht | daughter |
| knew | debt | knuckle | aisle | thorough |
| viscount | solemn | debris | isle | conscience |

## Game 1

■ Copy the words above onto individual word cards. Make cards for each of the letters **k**, **h**, **c**, **g**, **s**, **n**, **t** and **b**. Sort the words by silent letter.

## Game 2

You need a partner for this.

■ Mix up all the word and letter cards. Share out seven cards each.

■ The youngest player goes first by putting down a card, saying the word and the silent letter it has.

■ The next player has to follow with another card with the same silent letter.

■ If they cannot go, they must take a card from the pile until they can go.

■ If you have a letter card it can be used to switch the silent letter you are matching to any silent letter you want.

■ The game finishes when one player gets rid of all their cards.

Name:

# Silent letters

# Can you see it?

■ Fill in the silent letters and find the words in the word search.

■ Match the word pairs to show which words have the same silent letter.

| | | | |
|---|---|---|---|
| s__ience | debri__ | i__land | r__ythm |
| ca__m | __nat | __night | solem__ |
| cas__le | hym__ | lam__ | throu__ |
| crum__ | __nuckle | lis__en | cou__d |
| dau__ter | ve__icle | mus__le | __nome |

| d | n | u | g | f | e | l | t | v | f | g | q | m | e | q |
|---|---|---|---|---|---|---|---|---|---|---|---|---|---|---|
| q | a | f | k | m | d | h | g | n | q | l | k | t | c | a |
| h | g | u | o | r | h | t | t | c | e | q | z | h | n | e |
| p | r | n | g | i | s | l | a | n | d | f | h | g | e | z |
| l | g | i | y | h | d | s | v | e | h | k | c | i | i | w |
| c | o | u | l | d | t | e | b | b | l | y | v | n | c | x |
| u | v | h | f | l | h | e | b | p | k | c | m | k | s | w |
| v | z | t | e | i | l | m | r | r | g | d | s | n | y | s |
| b | u | c | c | k | a | p | y | n | i | m | u | u | g | o |
| m | v | l | j | n | m | o | a | e | h | s | o | x | m | l |
| u | e | r | u | u | b | t | f | t | r | v | k | h | x | e |
| r | m | l | a | c | w | f | y | n | e | t | s | i | l | m |
| c | m | r | o | k | i | h | u | f | a | z | t | u | f | n |
| a | g | v | p | l | r | m | i | h | f | s | k | d | c | l |
| m | d | l | i | e | a | d | u | p | s | e | y | o | e | g |

# Tricky words

## Objective

To understand that the spelling of some words needs to be learned specifically.

## Background knowledge

The purpose of this section is to provide you with some ideas of ways to deal with tricky words that children frequently use and often misspell. There are many tricky words in English because the language has evolved over hundreds of years. Some words have no particular rule to guide their spelling or pronunciation so it is important to give the children other tools they can use. You can strengthen visual memory by giving activities like filling in the missing tricky letters. Some will benefit from breaking the word into syllables and sounding it out, stressing each sound. Some children learn more effectively when they physically work with the word so let them cut it up and stick it back together or write it out. Extend the ideas in this section to cover the various learning styles so that everyone feels equipped to deal with these tricky words.

## Activities

● **Photocopiable page 96 'Don't stress it'**
There are many words with vowels that are difficult to hear because they are spoken quickly or quietly. When the stress falls on one syllable and not another, the vowel in the unstressed syllable is often not sounded when spoken aloud. Common instances of unstressed vowels can be found in words with the suffixes 'ary' and 'ory'. Also the letter strings 'er' and 'ed' are frequently unstressed. It can be helpful to get the children to say the words aloud and sound the unstressed letters.
● **Photocopiable page 97 'Syl-la-bi-fi-ca-tion'**
Using the technique of dividing words into syllables and sounds is particularly useful when spelling longer words with unstressed letters. Providing the children with plenty of practice in deconstructing and analysing the

spelling conventions of these types of words will help them to work out the most plausible spelling when they need to spell complex words. Breaking a word up into syllables with double letters and unstressed vowels, then pronouncing each syllable separately, will help children remember the right spelling by combining a visual and auditory image of the word.
● **Photocopiable page 98 'Tricky soundz'**
The children are helped to spell tricky words by being encouraged to identify the tricky sounds. Say a word and get them to identify the tricky sound. If the tricky sound is the /f/ sound, ask if they think it's like /f/ in *soft* or *coffee* or *phone*. This will help visual learners to associate words that have the same letter patterns.

## Further ideas

● **Sound hunt:** Give the children a sound like 's' and ask them to find as many words as possible with that sound but spelled in different ways like **s**un, dre**ss**, pur**s**e, **c**ell, **i**ce. You could give them a time limit of 2 minutes. Use more difficult words from the Year 5 and 6 word list.
● **Word break:** Give the children a number of cards with syllables taken from two or three words. In pairs, let them build words using the cards.
● **Word walk:** Let the children go outside and walk around in small groups of three or four. Each child gets a chance to choose a word and then everyone in the group takes a step for every letter in the word. Give them a destination and let them find out how many words it takes to get there.

## Digital content

On the digital component you will find:
● Printable versions of all three photocopiable pages.
● Answers to all three photocopiable pages.
● Interactive version of 'Don't stress it'.

Name:

## Tricky words

# Don't stress it

■ The ends of these words are unstressed. Find the correct ending for each word beginning and write the complete word next to the word beginning.

| ory | ery | ely | ary | ally | ed | er | ure |
|-----|-----|-----|-----|------|----|----|----|

■ Check your answers in a dictionary.

| | | | |
|-----|-----|-----|-----|
| categ | | equipp | |
| cemet | | privileg | |
| definit | | secret | |
| profession | | soldi | |
| especi | | temperat | |
| immediat | | necess | |
| desperat | | sincer | |
| attach | | should | |
| dramatic | | signat | |
| determin | | individu | |

■ Say each complete word aloud, stressing the end of the word so that it sounds quite different. This should help you to remember the word endings.

## Tricky words

# Syl-la-bi-fi-ca-tion

■ Make words by un-jumbling the syllables.

| gest | sug |
| --- | --- |

_____

| oc | py | cu |
| --- | --- | --- |

_____

| par | ap | ent |
| --- | --- | --- |

_____

| gres | sive | ag |
| --- | --- | --- |

_____

| ty | ni | mu | com |
| --- | --- | --- | --- |

_____

| com | ac | ny | pa |
| --- | --- | --- | --- |

_____

| sy | trov | con | er |
| --- | --- | --- | --- |

_____

| tion | ex | pla | na |
| --- | --- | --- | --- |

_____

| rupt | in | ter |
| --- | --- | --- |

_____

| mit | com | tee |
| --- | --- | --- |

_____

| mar | lous | vel |
| --- | --- | --- |

_____

| vous | mis | chie |
| --- | --- | --- |

_____

| pe | tion | com | ti |
| --- | --- | --- | --- |

_____

| com | date | mo | ac |
| --- | --- | --- | --- |

_____

| mun | ate | com | ic |
| --- | --- | --- | --- |

_____

| ci | nun | a | pro | tion |
| --- | --- | --- | --- | --- |

_____

■ On the back of this page, break the words below into syllables:

| symbol | opportunity | prejudice | recommend | temperature |
| --- | --- | --- | --- | --- |
| vegetable | according | system | develop | |

Name:

## Tricky words

# Tricky soundz

■ Can you hear the /z/ sound in each word below? Show which letters make this sound by writing the word in the correct letter box.

| buzz | bruise | criticise | disastrous | exaggerate |
| existence | recognise | physical | zip | sneeze |

| z | zz | ze | s | se | x |
|---|----|----|---|----|---|
|   |    |    |   |    |   |

■ Can you hear the /s/ sound in each word? Show which letters make this sound by writing the words below in the correct letter box.

| aggressive | cemetery | controversy | horse | convenience |
| curiosity | embarrass | excellent | existence | harass |
| hindrance | symbol | curse | purse | pronunciation |

| s | ss | se | c | ce |
|---|----|----|---|----|
|   |    |    |   |    |

■ Circle the common sound in these words:

| physical | sufficient | sacrifice | enough | definite |
| familiar | foreign | forty | interfere | trough |
| twelfth | dolphin | cough | | |

# Assessment

## Assessment grid

The following grid shows the main objectives and activities covered in this chapter. You can use the grid to locate activities that cover a particular focus that you are keen to monitor.

| Objective | Page | Activity title |
|---|---|---|
| To continue to distinguish between homophones and other words which are often confused. | 84 | Which one won? |
| | 85 | Write it right |
| | 86 | Homophone riddle |
| | 88 | Near homophones |
| | 89 | Apostrophe confusion |
| | 90 | What's my definition? |
| To spell some words with 'silent' letters. | 92 | Picture it |
| | 93 | Silent letter sort |
| | 94 | Can you see it? |
| To understand that the spelling of some words needs to be learned specifically. | 96 | Don't stress it |
| | 97 | Syl-la-bi-fi-ca-tion |
| | 98 | Tricky soundz |

## Observation and record keeping

Observe which children develop the ability to use the skills taught in this chapter to assist them with difficult spelling. When children ask for the spelling of words during independent writing, prompt them to identify the tricky part of the word – are there silent letters, tricky sounds or is the word a homophone? Encourage them to break the word into syllables and take note of children who still struggle with this. Keep a record of the most frequently misspelled words. Display these words so the class is aware of them. You can also encourage the children to keep their own spelling journal.

## Assessment activity

● **What you need**
Photocopiable page 100 'Listen well, spell well', writing materials, paper.

● **What to do**
Divide the class into two or three ability groups and explain that you are going to dictate a short passage which contains some words with tricky sounds. Read the passage to the children a couple of times. According to the ability level of the group, discuss the tricky words in the passage. Ask them to picture the word, can they identify the sounds and associate them with other words? Finally, do they know which words should be broken into syllables to assist with spelling? Explain that they should write the passage as you read it, breaking down difficult words into syllables.

## Differentiation

● Three dictation options are provided to enable the class to be divided by ability. More confident learners should attempt the first passage while less confident learners should use the second passage or the individual sentences. Prepare the children who are doing the more difficult one by giving them the other texts as a preliminary task. Children who do the easier dictation can use the difficult one as an extension activity.

## Further learning

● **Quiz:** Arrange the children into small mixed-ability groups to play against each other in a timed competition. Provide the children with whiteboards and pens. Read a tricky word aloud to the children without letting them see the written word. The group who all write the correct word on their boards in the shortest time wins.

Name:

# Assessment

# Listen well, spell well

In each dictation there are homophones, words with silent letters and unstressed sounds. Use your knowledge of tricky words and your syllabification skills to work out the correct spelling of these words.

### Dictation 1

The principal said that every Wednesday morning the whole school must attend a course on how to communicate sincerely in a foreign language. Those individuals who passed with excellent results would immediately proceed to the next level to further their skills.

(There are 15 to find.)

### Dictation 2

The soldier rode his horse like lightning across the desert to deliver the king's message. The prophet waited in the ancient cemetery to accept the secret diary bearing the physical symbol of the king.

(There are 12 to find.)

### Dictation 3

*Each sentence contains one homophone and a word with a silent letter.*

I heard the old man cough.
We'll need directions to the island.
You must have a license to go on the yacht.
Let's make a dessert for the new neighbour.
Please keep the receipt for the stationery.

(There are 10 to find.)

**PHOTOCOPIABLE**

# Chapter 6

# Improving your work

## Introduction

The opening section of this chapter aims to develop the children's dictionary skills and remind them that it can be used to check spelling as well as meanings. The chapter then delves into thesaurus work to help the children broaden their vocabulary. The children are encouraged to replace commonly used words with more interesting alternatives. The chapter moves on to focus on proofing for spelling errors, initially by reinforcing the process of identifying possible errors independently. The final activity in the section focuses once more on proofing for spelling errors but focusing on homophones, silent letters, tricky word endings and easily confused words. The final section challenges the children to propose changes to vocabulary to enhance effects and clarify meaning. For further practice, please see the 'Improving your work' section in the Year 5 workbook.

## In this chapter

| | |
|---|---|
| **Dictionary skills** page 103 | To use a dictionary to check the spelling and meaning of words. |
| **Using a thesaurus** page 107 | To use a thesaurus. |
| **Checking your work** page 111 | To proofread for spelling errors. |
| **Improving and extending vocabulary** page 115 | To propose changes to vocabulary to enhance effects and clarify meaning. |
| **Assessment** page 119 | Activities and ideas to assess spelling and vocabulary. |

## Poster notes

**Proof it! (page 102)**

The poster provides a checklist for proofreading and editing work independently. The poster can be enlarged and put on the wall to remind the children that proofing is essential. Use the poster to demonstrate that proofing is a process with different elements to it: spelling, punctuation and selecting the best vocabulary. The poster can also be used as a plenary when children have completed a piece of extended writing in any subject. It may be useful to laminate a copy for each table as a reminder for those children reluctant to go through the process.

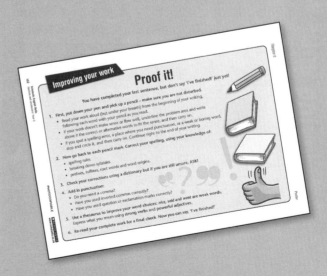

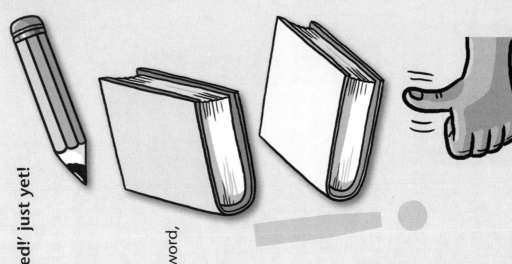

Improving your work

# Proof it!

You have completed your last sentence, but don't say 'I've finished!' just yet!

1. **First, put down your pen and pick up a pencil – make sure you are not disturbed.**
   - Read your work aloud (but under your breath) from the beginning of your writing, following each word with your pencil as you read.
   - If your work doesn't make sense or flow well, underline the problem area and write above it the correct or alternative words to fit the sense, and then carry on.
   - If you spot a spelling error, a place where you need punctuation, or a weak or boring word, stop and circle it, and then carry on. Continue right to the end of your writing.

2. **Now go back to each pencil mark. Correct your spelling, using your knowledge of:**
   - spelling rules
   - breaking down syllables
   - prefixes, suffixes, root words and word origins.

3. **Check your corrections using a dictionary but if you are still unsure, ASK!**

4. **Add in punctuation:**
   - Do you need a comma?
   - Have you used inverted commas correctly?
   - Have you used question or exclamation marks correctly?

5. **Use a thesaurus to improve your word choices:** *nice, said* and *went* are weak words. Express what you mean using strong verbs and powerful adjectives.

6. **Re-read your complete work for a final check. Now you can say, 'I've finished!'**

# Dictionary skills

### Objective

To use a dictionary to check the spelling and meaning of words.

### Background knowledge

Children need to be taught how to use a dictionary efficiently. In this section, the children use dictionaries to complete focused tasks to help them develop their understanding of the features and layout of a dictionary, as well as to increase their dexterity with grapheme–phoneme correspondence. There are many types of dictionaries at many different levels. However, the children should be introduced to the basic features and abbreviations used in the majority of cases. Draw the children's attention to how the class dictionary addresses parts of speech (verb, noun, adverb, adjective, article), meanings, abbreviations, antonyms and synonyms, compound words, derivatives and formal/informal words. Many dictionaries also include information on spelling of plurals and verb tenses, and provide help with pronunciation, which in turn, can assist with spelling. Children can use dictionaries to investigate root words and their derivatives, as well as prefixes. Some dictionaries contain etymological information.

### Activities

● **Photocopiable page 104 'Spelling Snakes and Ladders'**
Cut out the sets of words. Demonstrate with a volunteer how the game works. Let the volunteer ask you a word: first how to spell it – move on one place if correct; second, what the word means – move on another place if correct. Make sure the children have dictionaries available to check definitions. Explain that if they reach a square with a ladder, they move up the ladder – but if they land on a square with a snake head, they must go down. The words on the photocopiable sheet are in many cases words that do not always follow rules and just need to be learned. They can be replaced with any

set of words of your choice and the game can be used as an alternative to a spelling test. Children who find spelling challenging can work in pairs and give spelling clues, letter by letter.
● **Photocopiable page 105 'What is that word?'**
The children use their class dictionaries to establish what information their dictionary provides relating to the target words. They start by identifying and writing into the table both the word class and its definition. Check your class dictionary to establish what information it provides. Then, on the board, work through the first word on the sheet, demonstrating each element of additional information.
● **Photocopiable page 106 'Create a glossary'**
The children use the word banks provided to create a Science glossary of vocabulary for the Year 5 Programme of Study. A word-processing package can be used to organise the words into alphabetical order and for typing up the corresponding definitions. It may be useful to insert the words into a table. Let the children use a search engine to locate pictures to support their glossaries. Refer the children to their knowledge of root words to assist them in locating definitions and spellings of technical words.

### Further ideas

● **Technical glossary:** Encourage the children to create a glossary of technical terms at the end of units of work in other curriculum areas.
● **Dictionary pages:** Let the children make table-top, single-page dictionaries for younger year groups on the computer. Entries should be in alphabetical order and there should be a mixture of verbs, nouns and adjectives. When complete, laminate and present to the younger classes.

### Digital content

On the digital component you will find:
● Printable versions of all three photocopiable pages.
● Answers to 'What is that word?'.

Name:

## Dictionary skills

# Spelling Snakes and Ladders

■ Each player takes a set of words (or chooses their own). The players take turns. The *Asker* calls out a word. The *Responder* writes it down and gives it meaning.

■ The *Asker* checks in the dictionary. If the spelling is correct, the *Responder* moves forward one square. If the meaning is correct, the *Responder* moves on a second square.

■ The *Asker* may give clues by saying up to three letters in the word. Players move up ladders but down snakes.

| accommodate | curiosity | convenience | guarantee | occur |
| sufficient | restaurant | exaggerate | foreign | existence |
| frequently | twelfth | average | vegetable | available |
| amateur | hindrance | mischievous | bargain | embarrass |

| relevant | variety | language | government | immediate |
| ancient | nuisance | parliament | secretary | thorough |
| opportunity | recommend | queue | forty | committee |
| leisure | programme | awkward | neighbour | prejudice |

**PHOTOCOPIABLE**

Name:

# Dictionary skills

# What is that word?

■ Use a dictionary to identify the different word classes and definitions of the words below. Then include any other useful information which helps you spell the word and its related derivatives correctly.

■ Add in some tricky examples of your own.

| Word | Class | Definition | Extra information: past tense, plural, derivatives, origins, synonyms, antonyms |
|---|---|---|---|
| podium | | | |
| equipage | | | |
| automaton | | | |
| denounce | | | |
| assignation | | | |
| conscientious | | | |
| unbeknownst | | | |
| | | | |
| | | | |

Name:

# Dictionary skills

# Create a glossary

- Create a glossary of scientific terms using the word banks below.
- Arrange each bank of words into alphabetical order.
- Use a dictionary to find a definition for each word.

### Properties and changes of materials

condensation
evaporation
temperature
state
melt
freeze
irreversible
boiling point
magnetism
conductivity
transparency
solubility
hardness
solid
gas
thermometer
volume
properties
precipitation
liquid
sieve
dissolve
reversible

### Living things and their habitats

petal
carpal
dispersal
fruit
life-cycle
nutrients
ovary
ovule
photosynthesis
pollen
reproduce
seeds
germination
pollination
sepal
stamen
chlorophyll
stigma
fertilisation
tuber
environment

### Animals including humans

mammal
amphibian
insect
plants
animals
bird
puberty
gestation
life-cycle
digestive system
hormone
naturalist
animal behaviourist

### Earth and space

solar system
spherical
star
axis
celestial
rotate
access
atmosphere
orbit
shadow
moon
planet
Venus
Mercury
Mars
Jupiter
Saturn
Uranus
Neptune
geocentric
heliocentric
astronomical

### Forces

friction
parachute
pulleys
resistance
mechanism
gravity
lever
gear

### Scientific terms

science
scientific enquiry
scientifically
data
observation
variable
diagram
apparatus
equipment
classification
similarities
differences
measurement

**PHOTOCOPIABLE**

# Using a thesaurus

## Objective

To use a thesaurus.

## Background knowledge

A thesaurus provides alternative words with the same or similar meaning as the words being investigated: these are known as *synonyms*. A thesaurus also provides words with the opposite meaning to the focus word: these are called *antonyms*. A thesaurus, therefore, can assist with antonym spellings where negative prefixes are used. By looking up the word for which an antonym is required, children can identify whether they have used the correct spelling. Many thesauri also provide words that relate to a particular topic. The ability to use a thesaurus effectively is therefore a key tool in expanding vocabulary and improving writing standards. It is important that the children not only seek to use more interesting or powerful words but are also able to appreciate nuance, shades of meaning and connotation. In addition, it will help children select words that elucidate more accurately what they are trying to express.

## Activities

● **Photocopiable page 108 'Build your own word power'**
Provide the children with access to a thesaurus. Check they understand the difference between the role of a thesaurus and the role of a dictionary. Explain that a thesaurus is like a treasure chest – opening it unlocks a whole new world of words to make writing more descriptive, precise and powerful. Write the overused word *said* on the board. Invite volunteers to suggest synonyms and list them on the board, expanding the list if necessary (using an online thesaurus if possible). Discuss whether the words mean *nearly the same* or *exactly the same*.

● **Photocopiable page 109 'Strong synonyms and anti antonyms'**
Revise the role of a thesaurus by asking what it can provide (synonyms, antonyms, sometimes words related

to the topic). Discuss its importance (expand vocabulary, improve writing skills and so on). Give examples on the board of weak or ordinary verbs made more descriptive using adverbs (walk slowly: *stroll, amble, saunter*). Invite volunteers to replace example verbs and adverbs with single more powerful verbs (synonyms). Remind the children that opposites can be formed using prefixes (*happy – unhappy*) but that sometimes the antonym (opposite) is an entirely new word (*go – come*).

● **Photocopiable page 110 'Add to how was it said?'**
The activity involves sentences containing dialogue. Each has a space for an adverb that can qualify the verb. The children decide on an adverb that will fit each sentence, using the words from the box and having applied general spelling rules to turn them into adverbs. They then use a thesaurus to locate synonyms and antonyms for each adverb, recording their preferred choices in the box. Compile a class list of all the adverbs used and their synonyms.

## Further ideas

● **Word work:** Select a word of the day or week that you encounter a lot in the children's writing. Put up a poster with sections similar to those on photocopiable page 108, completing the definition and word class sections. Challenge the children to find synonyms during the week and antonyms if appropriate. Reward use of these words in their own writing.
● **Meet Roget:** Challenge some children by getting them to make a poster about Peter Mark Roget (of Roget's thesaurus) or draw up a personal profile on him.
● **Game time:** Make sets of synonym cards that the children can use to play happy families or even snap.

## Digital content

On the digital component you will find:
● Printable versions of all three photocopiable pages.
● Answers to 'Strong synonyms and anti antonyms' and 'Add to how it was said'.

Name:

## Using a thesaurus

# Build your own word power

■ Complete the table for each overused word. Use a dictionary to check the definition, but use a thesaurus to find synonyms. Then choose one of the synonyms to use in a sentence. The first word has been started for you.

| Word | Class | Definition | Synonyms |
|------|-------|------------|----------|
| very | adjective | emphasises an adjective or a verb | extremely, fantastically, … |

Sentence: _____

| | | | |
|------|-------|------------|----------|
| see | | | |

Sentence: _____

| | | | |
|------|-------|------------|----------|
| walk | | | |

Sentence: _____

| | | | |
|------|-------|------------|----------|
| happy | | | |

Sentence: _____

| | | | |
|------|-------|------------|----------|
| nice | | | |

Sentence: _____

| | | | |
|------|-------|------------|----------|
| went | | | |

Sentence: _____

**PHOTOCOPIABLE**

## Using a thesaurus

# Strong synonyms and anti antonyms

- ■ Read each sentence and choose a single verb from the mini thesaurus to replace the verbs and adverbs in bold.
- ■ Choose your favourite synonym verb to fit the context.

### MINI THESAURUS

pealed, boomed, clanged, knelled, tolled

bounded, bounced, leapt, sprang, hurtled

reprimanded, scolded, admonished, chastised

dashed, darted, rushed, scurried, nipped

flopped, crashed, collapsed, sagged, slumped

crept, snuck, sidled, slinked, skulked, tiptoed, crawled

Class 5 were **roundly told off** for talking in assembly. _____

The dog **came excitedly** into the room. _____

The lions **walked silently** through the bushes. _____

The twins **sat down exhaustedly** onto the beanbag. _____

The bells **rang out loudly** to mark the occasion. _____

Mr Lomax **ran quickly** to the shops to buy some milk. _____

- ■ Use your thesaurus to find an antonym for each word. Then choose two of your best antonyms and use them in a sentence.

disastrous _____      appreciate _____

achieve _____      definite _____

conscious _____      awkward _____

1. _____

2. _____

Name:

## Using a thesaurus

# Add to how it was said

■  Turn the words in the box into adverbs and use them to complete the sentences below. Try to pick the adverb that is the best fit for each sentence.

■  Use a thesaurus to find a synonym and an antonym for each adverb. Write them in the boxes underneath the sentences.

| furious | ecstatic | nervous | sleepy | gentle |

1. "Go to sleep, little one, and sweet dreams" whispered Mum _____ as she tucked my baby sister into bed.

| Synonym: | Antonym: |
|---|---|

2. "I will not tolerate receiving such dreadful work," bellowed the teacher _____ as he handed out last week's homework.

| Synonym: | Antonym: |
|---|---|

3. "Please don't hurt me!" begged the young boy _____ as the bully grabbed his school bag.

| Synonym: | Antonym: |
|---|---|

4. "We've won! We've won!" the team cheered _____ as the final whistle blew.

| Synonym: | Antonym: |
|---|---|

5. "It's been such a long day, I'm so tired!" declared Liam _____ as he snuggled under his bedcovers.

| Synonym: | Antonym: |
|---|---|

# Checking your work

## Objective

To proofread for spelling errors.

## Background knowledge

The children need to be taught to check their written work. Proofreading is an integral part of the writing process and should be valued as an opportunity to improve content. It is also an essential skill for eradicating careless spelling errors. Allocated time needs to be set aside to make editing and proofing a habit not a chore. It is important to highlight the importance of proofreading, not just as a requirement in school but as a life skill. Provide examples of where it is important to carry out checks of written work, such as in journalism. Checking work provides an excellent discussion forum on spelling rules and patterns. It also reveals to children personal common errors, which allows them to develop strategies to improve the quality of their writing. Encourage children to check each other's work. Children sometimes learn more from editing a partner's work than they do from editing their own.

## Activities

● **Photocopiable page 112 'YOU are the teacher'**
The children use a different coloured pen or pencil to mark a prepared piece of work. Explain that they should read the work aloud, while following with their pen, to help identify spelling mistakes. Encourage them to identify as many errors as they can independently – perhaps circling ones they are sure of and underlining ones they would like to check. They can then work with a partner to check their words (first with each other and then in the dictionary). Invite volunteers in the plenary to suggest helpful spelling rules and challenging words to learn.

● **Photocopiable page 113 'Proof it'**
The children can use this page to log and investigate spelling errors from pieces of their own work. They use the prompts to help assess why the spelling is incorrect and what strategies they can use to make corrections.

Use the log as a guide for a plenary or introductory session to revise spelling rules. Encourage ongoing use of the log.

● **Photocopiable page 114 'Hard choices'**
The children are proofreading for errors once more but this time their focus is homophones, silent letters, tricky word endings and easily confused words. The most important thing is context because the word choices are either homophones or have been written phonetically with an incorrect choice of grapheme. Allow them to work independently or with a partner to circle the correct choice of word before sharing the passage in a plenary.

## Further ideas

● **Help a friend:** Encourage peer assessment where opportunities arise. The children challenge each other to find mistakes in their work before handing it in for marking. They often learn more from looking at another's work.

● **Pear, pare, pair:** Have regular challenges on which homophone to choose in different contexts. Invent a sentence and ask for volunteers to say how the focus word should be spelled. Do two or three as warm ups to lessons. Encourage the children to set each other challenges too.

● **Hit-list spelling:** Encourage each child to have a weekly 'hit list' of 5–10 words they have difficulty spelling – words can stay on the list or fall off when mastered. Each time they spell a hit-list word correctly or independently correct one, they can underline the word and keep a tally on their hit list. Invent rewards for words they master.

## Digital content

On the digital component you will find:
● Printable versions of all three photocopiable pages.
● Answers to 'YOU are the teacher' and 'Hard choices'.
● Interactive versions of 'YOU are the teacher' and 'Hard choices'.

## Checking your work

# YOU are the teacher

■ Use a coloured pencil to mark Leon's work. Can you find at least 30 spelling mistakes? Write the correct spellings in the margin.

■ Can you suggest any spelling rules that Leon should remember?

■ Can you point out any exception words that you just need to learn to spell?

**Tip:** Make a note of spellings to learn in your notebook.

|  | |
|---|---|
|  | Munday 1 Febrary<br><br>My best day ever!<br>by Leon Proctor<br><br>Last Saterday I played soccer in our comunity cup final. It was a very importunt game and I was nervus. I am the goalie so I'm always consious of everyone staring at me, desperatly hoping I can stop the ball hiting the back of the net. We arrived at the feild at 10 o'clock and joged round the pich to warm up. The opposition were all in green and looked as thow they ment buisness. They'd had an excelent season up to the final and were just as determinned to win as we were.<br>The whisle bloo and the game began. Their striker was quick as lightening with huge mussles. After just five minuits, he got a corner right on the edge of the opposition box. Despite a powerfull kick, the ball hit the post and I cleared it away. Lucky! An early goal would have been disastrus for morale! By half time, it was one all.<br>In the second harf, I saved a second goal but the ball hit me rihgt in the face – big broose and black eye tomorrow! The game got really tense as time was runing out – it was necessry to up our game if we were going to win the competishun cup and meddals. After an awkwad cross from Tim, Colin picked up the ball and despite being seriously harrassed by their captin, managed to slip the ball past their keeper just as the final wissle went after fourty minnits. What an achievment! I'm not exagerating when I say it was my best day ever! |

Name:

## Checking your work

# Proof it

■ Use this sheet to log the spelling errors in your work and identify why the error was made. Try to record your personal spelling challenges and use it to check your progress. Add to it whenever you can.

| Word | Wrong plural rule | Forgot to double the consonant | Forgot to change y to i | Forgot to drop the e | Other (eg wrong homophone) | Correct spelling |
|------|------|------|------|------|------|------|
| | | | | | | |
| | | | | | | |
| | | | | | | |
| | | | | | | |
| | | | | | | |
| | | | | | | |
| | | | | | | |
| | | | | | | |
| | | | | | | |
| | | | | | | |

**PHOTOCOPIABLE**

Name:

## Checking your work

# Hard choices

■ Mhairi has identified possible spelling errors in her letter. Using the context in the letter, circle the correctly spelled word for her to use.

**Tip:** Check for homophones, silent letters, tricky word endings and easily confused words.

Class 5B
Hill Lane Primary
Bishop Lavis
BL7 4HD

Dear Editor

We **wood/would** like to ask **weather/whether** you would publish **ann/an** article in your newspaper about a **pair/pear** of Year 5 children raising money for charity.

**Won/One mourning/morning** last **week/weak**, **too/two** of **our/hour** school's Year 5s, Alison and Meegan, began their **accent/ascent** of Scafell Pike to **raze/raise** money **four/for** charity. They **were/where** half **whey/way** up when they decided to take a rest, being a bit out of **breathe/breath** with legs feeling like **led/lead**. While sitting in the **son/sun** and looking at the view, the girls **heard/herd** a pitiful cry. They investigated to **insure/ensure** that it wasn't anything to worry about and **saw/sore** a dog caught up in **steal/steel** wire. They tried to **prise/prize** the dog **lose/loose** but couldn't get the wire **of/off** the dog's **feat/feet**.

Eventually they persuaded the dog to calm down and **weight/wait** patiently **while/wile** they untangled the **why're/wire**. They **rapped/wrapped** the dog in **their/there** coats and Alison carried him down with his head **peaking/peeking** out of her backpack. When they reached the bottom, they went **straight/strait** to the closest vet, who gave the dog a **bowel/bowl** of **serial/cereal** to give him strength. The vet said he would keep the lost dog as a **guessed/guest** until the girls found **hymn/him** a new home. "**Weave/ We've** decided to donate the money raised to **sett/set** up an animal rescue shelter," said the girls. "We **no/know** we can't **altar/alter** what has happened but we can change the future. Please help us make a **diffrence/ difference**."

If you want to know more, please contact our school **principal/principle**.

Yours faithfully
Mhairi

PHOTOCOPIABLE

# Improving and extending vocabulary

## Objective

To propose changes to vocabulary to enhance effects and clarify meaning.

## Background knowledge

We often understate or overstate situations through our choice of vocabulary. Sometimes an adjective fails to provide meaningful description: *This book was really good*! 'Good' says little about the book. In other circumstances we might over-exaggerate a situation: *The sea is absolutely freezing!* Obviously it is not literally freezing. While *distinctly chilly* might be more precise, the children need to differentiate where exaggeration or persuasiveness may or may not be in order. The children's writing is often initially littered with commonly overused words such as 'said' and 'nice' – as well as being dull, such words are somewhat imprecise. Many children also choose weak verbs, such as *went*. To communicate more effectively, help the children find interesting alternatives that reflect what they really mean: in doing so, they need to be mindful of the purpose and audience for a piece of writing as it affects the type and level of language to be used.

## Activities

● **Photocopiable page 116 'A superior word to "said"'**
Discuss how often 'said' appears in dialogue. List alternatives to *said* using the box words as a stimulus. The children should then work independently through the activity choosing appropriate synonyms for the verb – either from their box or from a thesaurus – to fill the spaces to enhance the effect of the sentences. As a plenary discuss how using the verb 'said' in conjunction with adverbs (such as *softly*, *quietly* and *angrily*) is an alternative way of expressing how dialogue is being conveyed.

● **Photocopiable page 117 'The Tortoise and the Hare'**
'The Tortoise and the Hare' is presented in simple language. The word bank provides synonyms for the verbs, adjectives, adverbs and nouns in the story. Discuss the meanings of these synonyms, referring to shades of meaning and how they add to the effect. Ask the children to rewrite the story for an older audience, incorporating some of the vocabulary provided.

● **Photocopiable page 118 'Choosing persuasive vocabulary'**
Carefully chosen words and phrases make a big difference when writing to persuade an audience. The children must improve on a letter asking a resident to keep the Youth Club running. They must be persuasive, but polite. Explain that they replace the bold sections with more meaningful alternatives – either single words or a phrases. Give an example (ask: *implore*, *urgently request*). More confident learners can add further information to persuade the recipient. Select children to read their letters aloud with others choosing the most persuasive letter, giving their reasons why.

## Further ideas

● **Notices:** Encourage the children to write notices and memos, selecting appropriate vocabulary to create the intended impact. For example, a police notice warning people about the need to conserve water.
● **Paint it for me:** Ask the children to write a description of a famous painting for a younger child and then rewrite it for an older person using a thesaurus to source more adventurous vocabulary.
● **Making changes:** Provide pairs of children with a purpose for a persuasive talk, such as not wanting to have any homework. Suggest different audiences for each pair, such as teachers, the class or their parents.

## Digital content

On the digital component you will find:
● Printable versions of all three photocopiable pages.
● Answers to 'A superior word to "said"' and 'Choosing persuasive vocabulary'.

Name:

# A superior word to "said"

■ The word *said* is easy to use but a bit dull. Liven up your dialogue by making more ambitious word choices.

■ Use a thesaurus or your own knowledge to add to the synonyms for *said* in the box. Then use the context to choose an appropriate but descriptive word to use instead of *said* in each sentence.

| announced | bellowed | commented | boasted |
|---|---|---|---|
| | muttered | declared | sniffed |

1. "I've got a terrible cold and I can't stop sneezing," ___sniffed___ Sam, reaching for yet another tissue.

2. "The mmmonster – it's cccoming to ggget us!" _____ the trio as they turned and fled the swamp.

3. The policeman shook his finger at the children, "Don't ever go near that railway embankment again," he _____.

4. "I've got so much homework," _____ Lisa, "I just won't have time to go to Jen's party."

5. The principal _____, "There will be a non-uniform day next Friday to raise money for charity."

6. "Get off my land!" _____ the farmer furiously.

7. "We're going to have another baby," _____ Dad, "and you're going to have a baby brother!"

8. "Our team is top of the league," Danny _____. "We are the best in the county!"

9. Pulling up alongside the village postman, the tourist _____, "Can you direct me to the Grand Hotel, please?"

**Improving and extending vocabulary**

# The Tortoise and the Hare

■ Rewrite this story in your own words for an older audience, choosing alternatives from the word bank below.

Once upon a time, there was a big-headed hare who boasted about how fast he could run. The tortoise, who was fed up of hearing the hare talk about how great he was, asked him to have a race.

"Even though you are so fast, I will beat you!" said the tortoise. The hare, thinking the tortoise was mad, agreed to the race.

All the animals from the forest came to the starting line to watch.

"Ready, steady, go!" The hare sprinted away from the start line and was off down the road, while the tortoise walked along slowly and steadily.

Turning to see the tortoise moving so slowly, so far behind him, the hare lay down by the side of the path and fell asleep, thinking to himself, "There's plenty of time for a rest."

Meanwhile, the tortoise carried on walking, slowly and steadily, never stopping until he reached the finish line. The animals cheered so loudly that the hare was woken from his sleep. He got up and began to sprint towards the finish but it was too late. The slow, steady tortoise had already won the race.

The moral of the story is, slow but steady wins the race.

| | |
|---|---|
| **Verbs** | to ridicule, to be exasperated, to challenge, to affirm, to assent, to believe, to trudge, to continue, to persevere, to rouse |
| **Adjectives** | conceited, agile, incredible, swift, jubilant, raucous, victorious |
| **Adverbs** | resolutely, doggedly, comfortable, haughtily, relentlessly, promptly |
| **Nouns** | assertion, proposal, slumber, snooze, ovation, applause |

■SCHOLASTIC
www.scholastic.co.uk          **PHOTOCOPIABLE**                                        **Scholastic English Skills**
                                                                                        Spelling and vocabulary: Year 5     **117**

Name:

# Choosing persuasive vocabulary

■ Rewrite this letter in your best handwriting, choosing new vocabulary to replace the words and phrases in bold to make it more persuasive.

■ When choosing words or phrases, remember that if your letter sounds too extreme you may upset the recipient. If you are too reasonable or timid, you may have no impact at all.

63 Conifer Lane
Lower Hillside
Shottesford
CV43 3GY

28 February 2015

Dear Mr Bruce

I am writing on behalf of all the children in the village of Lower Hillside to  you to  about closing down our youth club.

Closure of the youth club would be a  for the children as it them somewhere warm and safe to . We  that running the youth club involves time, effort and cost but we are prepared to  each week and to  to help the club run smoothly by clearing away and washing up – we could organise a  each week.

We hope that you  the effect that  this  would have on the village children?

We  you to  about your decision to close the club and to  to that will  for both sides.

We look forward to your  to .


From

Charlie Forrester

PHOTOCOPIABLE

# Assessment

## Assessment grid

The following grid shows the main objectives and activities covered in this chapter. You can use the grid to locate activities that cover a particular focus that you are keen to monitor.

| Objective | Page | Activity title |
|---|---|---|
| To use a dictionary to check the spelling and meaning of words. | 104 | Spelling Snakes and Ladders |
| | 105 | What is that word? |
| | 106 | Create a glossary |
| To use a thesaurus. | 108 | Build your own word power |
| | 109 | Strong synonyms and anti antonyms |
| | 110 | Add to how it was said |
| To proofread for spelling errors. | 112 | YOU are the teacher |
| | 113 | Proof it |
| | 114 | Hard choices |
| To propose changes to vocabulary to enhance effects and clarify meaning. | 116 | A superior word to "said" |
| | 117 | The Tortoise and the Hare |
| | 118 | Choosing persuasive vocabulary |

## Observation and record keeping

It is easy for children to only use words that are within their comfort zone. Conversely, some children are excited by new words and use them regardless of appropriate context. Use the spelling log to record the categories of spelling rules being missed and then assist each child to make a spelling plan. You can use spelling bees to observe progress. Keep challenging children to develop their word power and note which children are independently beginning to replace commonly used words with words with more muscle. Keep prompting children who use a small word range, perhaps by improving words of a particular class one at a time.

## Assessment activity

- **What you need**
Photocopiable page 120 'Working on wording' for each child, writing materials, dictionaries and thesauri.
- **What to do**
Briefly discuss the purpose of a school fair announcement. Point out that parents and other visitors would not be impressed by a school announcement full of mistakes. Explain that this announcement is a first draft and they have been asked to improve it. Make sure that the children understand that the activity has two parts: checking for errors (there are 35 in total), and then improving the effect of the announcement by using more powerful words to make it more persuasive.

## Differentiation

- Set different target levels of words to find and correct for children who struggle with spelling or reduce the amount to cover for slow readers by asking them to focus on just one column. In the same vein, challenge more able learners by setting time limits.
- More confident learners could be challenged to add further information and examples to the letter to make it more persuasive.

## Further learning

- **Class dictionary/thesaurus:** Use A3 or A2 card and marker pens. Allow one page per letter (or a double page spread for more common letters) and build up the resource in conjunction with the class. Include aspirational words, subject-specific words and so on. Invite children to add to it at appropriate moments.

**Assessment**

# Working on wording

■ Proofread this school announcement. Cross out any errors and write the correction above (there are 34 errors in total).

■ Then, underline at least 5 dull or overused words and phrases, and add more interesting alternatives above.

### CALLING ALL SPRINGERS!

The Springfield School summer fare will be on Saturday, 15 August. It is our biggest fundraising oportunity – so we appeal to all Springer families to help us make it a big success.

Our head girl will have the priviledge of introducing our importent guest, reknowned childrens author, May Tellatale, who will open the event at two o'clock. She will gladly sign copies of her knew interesting mistry, 'The Word that Woke the World' for evryone who waits and cues up. Their will be a fun bouncy casle and a real-life fire engin. There will also be intresting, fun shows with a magicion and a snake handle.

Please support our fun-picked day: wonder round the cake and book stalls to get a bargin, or drink a cup of tee at our 'Every Cup Counts Café' while lissning to the school choir as you sit down.

Don't forget the fun famly races and games, so bring your trainners! In the mislikely event of unclement weather, most things will moves to the scool hall but it would be sensible to bring an umbrela.

Please suport our great fair – bring your frends two. We are determinned to make this our best fair ever!

Entrie fee: £2 for adults; every one els is free.

**Scholastic English Skills**
120 Spelling and vocabulary: Year 5                    PHOTOCOPIABLE     ■SCHOLASTIC
www.scholastic.co.uk

# Glossary

**apostrophe:** Apostrophes have two uses – to show missing letters (such as *don't*) and to show possession. In singular nouns they are placed before the 's' (for example, *cat's*), in regular plural nouns they are placed after the 's' (*cats'*) but in irregular plural nouns they can be in either place (*children's*).

**compound:** A compound word contains at least two root words in its morphology; together, the words form a new word. Compounds can be separate words or joined, either with or without a hyphen: *cupboard*, *English teacher*, *ice-cream*.

**consonant:** The 21 letters of the alphabet that are not **vowels** ('a', 'e', 'i', 'o', 'u').

**etymology:** A word's etymology is its history: its origins in earlier forms of English or other languages, and how its form and meaning have changed.

**grapheme–phoneme correspondences (GPC):** The links between letters or combinations of letters (graphemes), and the speech sounds (phonemes) they represent. In the English writing system, graphemes may correspond to different phonemes in different words.

**grapheme:** A letter, or combination of letters, corresponding to a single phoneme within a word.

**homophone:** Words that sound the same but have different meanings and are spelled differently. Near-homophones are words that sound almost the same and are often confused (for example, *accept/except*, *affect/effect*).

**hyphen:** A punctuation mark used to join words (*co-production* and *first-hand*).

**morpheme:** The smallest unit of language with its own meaning: either a word or part of a word.

**morphology:** The internal make-up of a word in terms of root words, suffixes and prefixes, as well as changes such as *mouse* to *mice*. Morphology may be used to produce different inflections of the same word (*boy – boys*), or entirely new words (*boy – boyish*) in the same word family.

**phoneme:** One of the smallest units of speech (sound) that make one word different from another word. English has around 44 phonemes. One, two, three or four letters may represent a single phoneme, constituting a single grapheme.

**phrase:** A phrase is a group of words that are grammatically connected so that they stay together, and that expand a single word.

**plural:** More than one. Nouns are usually made plural by adding 's' or 'es', although there are irregular nouns with different pluralisation (such as *oxen, sheep, wolves*).

**possessive:** Words that show ownership. They may use the apostrophe in singular or plural forms (*Dad's car, Dads' cars*), or be personal possessive pronouns such as *mine, yours*.

**prefix:** A prefix is added to the beginning of a word to make another word, such as *regular/irregular*.

**root word:** A word that stands alone – *form* is the root word for other words in its word family (*inform, formation, reform*) and for its inflections (*forms, formed, forming*).

**silent letter:** Silent letters are not heard when pronouncing a word, but are there when it is written.

**suffix:** Suffixes are added at the end of root words to change them into another word, such as *danger/dangerous*. Sometimes the addition of a suffix changes the spelling of the root word (for example, *angry/angrily*). Suffixes cannot stand alone.

**syllable:** Words consist of one or more syllables. They are like the beats of a word and can be counted – for example, *word* has one syllable, *sentence* has two. Syllables have at least one vowel and possibly one or more consonants.

**vowel:** A speech sound produced without closure or obstruction of the vocal tract. Vowels can form syllables by themselves, or they combine with consonants. In the English writing system, the letters 'a', 'e', 'i', 'o', 'u' and 'y' can represent vowels.

**word class:** Every word belongs to a word class that summarises the ways in which it can be used in grammar, the major classes being: noun, verb, adjective, adverb, preposition, determiner, pronoun, conjunction. Word classes are also called 'parts of speech'.

**word family:** The words in a word family are normally related to each other by a combination of morphology, grammar and meaning.

# Word bank

This word bank, offers differentiated examples of vocabulary related to spelling patterns covered in the book. Each word bank links loosely to the contents of a chapter in the book and aims to support the learning of the vocabulary in each chapter. Together with the posters that accompany each chapter, they help prepare the children for their written work and formal assessments.

Words from the bank could be displayed as target words to enrich independent writing. You can also use them for dictionary work opportunities or word games such as hangman. In groups, the children can take turns to teach a set of words to their peers, or let them work in pairs and test one another using white boards or chalk. To test the children's competency, these words can be used to write or complete sentences, as well as for more formal dictation exercises and spelling tests.

Encourage the children to interact with this word bank by adding related words in their books. Once familiar with a word, let the children 'bank it' by highlighting the word or ticking it off the list.

## Revisit and reinforce                                                Chapter 1

| Basic | Intermediate | Advanced |
|---|---|---|
| unhappy | disagree | illegal |
| unpleasant | distasteful | dissatisfied |
| unable | misinterpret | immortal |
| unreliable | misunderstand | immature |
| unsociable | antisocial | irrational |
| unenthusiastic | anticlockwise | irresponsible |

## Suffixes and prefixes                                                Chapter 2

| Basic | | Intermediate | | Advanced | |
|---|---|---|---|---|---|
| fabricate | deaden | mummify | mesmerise | bidden | glamorise |
| hyphenate | strengthen | notify | fertilise | redden | legitimise |
| assassinate | lengthen | purify | immortalise | madden | quantify |
| authorise | blacken | intensify | colonise | sadden | mystify |
| characterise | loosen | falsify | economise | widen | horrify |
| standardise | deepen | beautify | pasteurise | pollinate | terrify |
| symbolise | lessen | glaciate | scrutinise | incinerate | electrify |
| equalise | dehydrate | activate | re-ask | calibrate | clarify |
| socialise | oxygenate | privatise | co-own | differentiate | liquefy |
| legalise | mislead | apologise | re-enact | accommodate | stupefy |
| dramatise | misunderstand | memorise | re-examine | aerate | identify |
| solidify | dishearten | categorise | re-enter | exemplify | electrify |
| justify | disappoint | sympathise | mis-say | televise | mortify |

## Word endings                                                   Chapter 3

| Basic | Intermediate | Advanced |
|---|---|---|
| space – spacious | fiction – fictitious | conscientious |
| caution – cautious | benefit – beneficial | facetious |
| office – official | palace – palatial | surreptitious |
| essence – essential | suspect – suspicious | scrumptious |
| rely – reliance | commerce – commercial | rambunctious |
| absent – absence | finance – financial | anxious |

## Word families, roots and origins                               Chapter 4

| Basic | Intermediate | Advanced |
|---|---|---|
| man, mannish | benefactor | septuagenarian |
| sad, saddish | chronicle | aqueduct |
| paragraph, autograph, | millennium | aquifer |
| geography, graphic | unnecessary | perimeter |
| anchor | anthropology | philharmonic |
| orchestra | punctuation | acupuncture |
| technology | spectacular | ignition, igneous |
| architect | explain, explanation | interrupt |
| chandelier | persuade, persuasion | spectator |
| parachute | system, systematic | morphology |
| cliché | energy, energetic | dodecahedron |
| sachet | fact, factual | memory, memorial, |
| cachet | sign, resign, signature, | immemorial, memorable, |
| gourmet | significant, assignation, | memorandum, |
| bouquet | designate | remembrance, |
| cornet | legal, legislation, legitimise | commemorate |

## Homophones and other tricky words                                          Chapter 5

| Basic | Intermediate | Advanced |
|---|---|---|
| freight (silent 'g') | draught ('f' sound) | secretary (unstressed 'ary') |
| yacht (silent 'c') | microphone ('f' sound) | equipped (unstressed 'ed') |
| vehicle (silent 'h') | cereal ('s' sound) | especially (unstressed 'ally') |
| island (silent 's') | cemetery ('s' sound) | category (unstressed 'ory') |
| solemn (silent 'n') | criticise ('z' sound) | stationery (unstressed 'ery') |
| succumb (silent 'b') | existence ('z' sound) | sincerely (unstressed 'ely') |

## Improving your work                                                         Chapter 6

| Basic | Intermediate | Advanced |
|---|---|---|
| ancient | thorough | queue |
| foreign | immediate | nuisance |
| forty | recommend | neighbour |
| awkward | twelfth | occurrence |
| programme | committee | restaurant |
| opportunity | conscience | exaggerate |
| sieve | ecstatic | privilege |
| environment | opportunity | guarantee |
| mechanism | heliocentric | embarrass |
| atmosphere | geocentric | chlorophyll |
| sidled | business | photosynthesis |
| crept | lightning | mischievous |
| mourning/morning | serial/cereal | accent/ascent/assent |
| meddle/medal | rapped/wrapped | perseverance |

# General activities

## How to use the general activities

This part of the book contains a variety of games and activities that can be generic ways of exploring work covered in the book. You may wish to use these activities as part of your spelling routine, or at other times with groups or the whole class. They are designed to be fast-paced activities for reinforcing or assessing spelling and extending vocabulary. The five-minute ideas can also be used as warm-ups or plenaries.

### Yes or no

**Linked activities:**
Any spellings in the book.

**What to do**
- Use this activity to focus on a specific set of target words, which the children are aware they are focusing on, for example, the week's spelling homework or a group of subject words.
- Organise the class into two teams, with half the class in each.
- Each group chooses a different person to represent it for each round of the game.
- Give each representative a word on a piece of paper that the others cannot see (from the target words). Without showing the word to anyone, or spelling the word, the representative must describe the word to their group, using clues like 'it has a prefix', 'it has three syllables', 'it's a noun', 'it's an opposite' or 'it sounds like…'.
- When the clues are finished the rest of the group can ask 'yes/no' questions, like 'Does it have five letters?' or 'Is the prefix 'un'?'
- Set a time limit for working out the word (a point can be given for each word. If no one has guessed it when the time is up, the representative writes the word on the board for everyone to see. The group with the most points wins the game.
- The groups can either observe each other in action or work in parallel, each with its own word challenge.

### Word scramble

**Linked activities:**
Any spellings in the book.

**What to do**
- Prepare sets of letter cards for different words (a group of target words), with each letter written clearly on a separate card (about the size of a postcard). Each set of letters should spell a different word.
- Organise the children into groups of four or five. Use the hall or a large space for teams to spread out. Give each group one set of cards, face-down on the floor.
- When the signal is given, the groups turn over their letters and unscramble them to form a word.
- The first group to complete its word stands up in a line holding the letters so they are visible to the rest of the class.
- As soon as a group completes a word, the other groups stop and their letter cards get passed on to another group and the next round begins. The successful group each time gets a fresh set of cards.
- The group who makes the most words wins the game.
- You can adapt this activity by focusing on a specific spelling focus, in which case you would tell the children that the scrambled words all have a particular sound, common letter string or meaning.

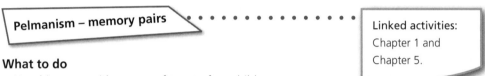

**Colour alert**

Linked activities: Any spellings in the book.

**What to do**

Provide each child with their list of spellings for homework and
challenge them to learn their spellings in a creative way. They could:
● write out each word using a different colour or bubble writing for the target letter
string.
● use a bright colour as an alert for unstressed or silent letters, for example, silent 'b'
could be in red or unstressed inflexional endings could be purple.
● write the words in a different colour of the rainbow for each day they practise
their spellings.

**Pelmanism – memory pairs**

Linked activities: Chapter 1 and Chapter 5.

**What to do**

● Use this game with groups of two to four children.
● Provide each child with 20 blank cards, approximately 6cm × 3cm.
● Invite the children to list ten pairs of homophones on a whiteboard or piece of paper.
Ask them to check the spellings, then write one word on each card.
● The children place the cards face down, spread out on the table.
● The first player turns over two cards in the position they were found in. If they have
found a pair of homophones, they keep the pair. If the cards are not a pair, they are turned
back over and the next player takes their turn.
● Play continues until all the pairs have been found. The winner is the player with the most
pairs of homophones.
● This game could also be adapted for homographs (bark: the noise a dog makes or the
outer covering of a tree). When an identical pair of words is found, the player can only
keep them if they can use them in sentences to show the different meanings. Each group
could have a dictionary for checking.

**Circle spell**

Linked activities: Links to all chapters.

**What to do**

● This activity provides practice in spelling words containing target
letter strings and is suitable for a whole-class activity.
● Prepare cards each containing a specific letter string, prefix, suffix or phoneme that
the class is working on. Place these face down in the middle of the circle.
● The class sits in a circle with a chosen child holding a beanbag.
● The first card is turned over and the player calls out and then spells a word containing
that letter string.
● They then throw the beanbag to another player who has to call and spell a different
word containing the same letter string.
● Play continues until a player calls change. They then turn over another card and play
continues with the new spelling focus.

Five-minute ideas

### Hangman

● Although an old favourite, hangman is a great warm-up activity and works especially well for words that just need to be learned, words with unstressed syllables or silent letters. It also works for certain letter strings or word endings, especially if you do a word or two each day.
● Choose a target word and write dashes on the board to represent each letter. The children suggest letters that might be in the word. If the guess is wrong, you start to draw the hangman – one line at a time.

### Brain boxes

● Draw four boxes and give each one a heading for a focus letter or word element such as: letter patterns, silent letters, prefixes, suffixes and so on.
● In pairs or small groups (on paper), or as a whole class (on the board), ask the children to fill the boxes with as many words as they can think of containing the focus letter or word element. The pair or group with the most letters score points. You could have a running tally chart on the wall. Allow the children to use a dictionary to check their spelling and correct them if necessary.

### Mix 'n' match

● Provide the children with selected prefix and suffix cards. Then hand out a set of word roots – they could be a standalone words for example 'love' or 'stems', especially from Latin and Greek, like 'spec' (*inspect*).
● Invite the children to race each other to create new words using the cards.

### Word chains

● Organise the class into circles (either in groups or as a whole-class activity).
● Each child must add a word to a word chain that goes around the circle following a criteria. Each child going round the chain must add a word to the chain that fits the criteria. When no more words can be added, the person who managed the last word scores a point.
● Appoint an adjudicator. The adjudicator's role is to check in the dictionary if there is a dispute about whether a word belongs in a chain. (You will need one adjudicator per group.)
● The criteria for the word chains could be anything to do with spelling patterns or vocabulary extension. This type of chain is more about word association and grouping than spelling. Add your own words to the chain to extend the level of difficulty.

### Zigzag

● This game is similar to word chains but the aim is to change the direction of the chain by using a homophone's (or homograph's) alternate meaning, for example: *kennel*, *canine*, *bark* – *tree*, *root* – *parsnip*, *carrot*, *swede*, *Norway* and so on.
● The game can be made easier by putting a list of homophones on the board and challenging the children to connect them via a word chain.

### Match that

● Use this game to explore homophones. Make cards of words that are homophones. Invite the children to work in pairs, taking turns to pick a card. The child who picks the card, says the word and puts it in context. For example: *sauce – The chicken came with a delicious sauce on the side.* The other child has to give the homophone putting it in context, for example: *source: Some people say the source of the River Thames is a spring called Thames Head in Gloucestershire, others say it is Seven Springs near Cheltenham.*